WATERSID
In Berk

Nick Channer

COUNTRYSIDE BOOKS
NEWBURY, BERKSHIRE

COUNTRYSIDE BOOKS
3 Catherine Road
Newbury, Berkshire

ISBN 1 85306 569 2

Designed by Graham Whiteman
Cover illustration by Colin Doggett
Photographs and maps by the author

Produced through MRM Associates Ltd., Reading
Printed by Woolnough Bookbinding Ltd., Irthlingborough

Contents

Walk

AREA MAP SHOWING THE LOCATION OF THE WALKS

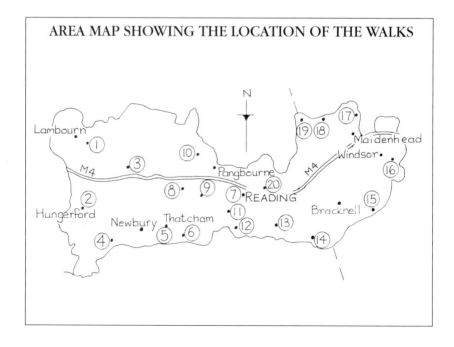

INTRODUCTION

Berkshire was never a large county but it became even smaller following the 1974 county boundary changes. However, within its borders lies a variety of scenery – from the remains of the ancient Windsor Forest in the east to the great sweeps of windswept downland in the west. In between there are gentle river valleys and some of the prettiest countryside in the south of England.

The walks in this book, all of which are circular and include full route-finding instructions, are designed to provide a unique insight into the changing character of the county's rural landscape. But hopefully they do much more than that. The one thing all the routes have in common is that they follow stretches of Berkshire's historic waterways. In the west of Berkshire you can take a stroll beside the Pang, one of the prettiest of the county's rivers; discover the partly hidden course of the Enborne; or follow the meandering Lambourn as it shelters beneath bare, exposed hills that seem more reminiscent of neighbouring Wiltshire than Berkshire. To the east, there is the chance to discover pretty Thatcher's Ford on the River Blackwater, enjoy a tour of man-made Virginia Water in Windsor Great Park, and seek out the hidden backwaters of Reading.

You can amble, too, along the towpath of the Kennet & Avon Canal which runs through much of the county and survives as a lasting monument to the engineering achievements of the pre-railway age, or take a walk along the Thames Path which follows the river along the county boundary and is a journey of endless delights, illustrating how the majestic Thames has shaped the landscape over the centuries.

Most of the walks in the book begin and finish at a local inn and all are easily manageable, undemanding routes. You don't have to be a serious walker or a hardy hiker to tackle them. However, there are often patches of wet ground to be found – even on a walk of 2 or 3 miles – and appropriate footwear is always an important consideration when out walking. A small rucksack to carry rainwear is recommended for the walk too, as is a copy of the relevant Ordnance Survey map, useful if you want to extend the route and for identifying the main features of views. A camera is also worth carrying as waterside walks often reveal plenty of wildlife and other fascinating attractions.

The pubs chosen for this book are genuine, authentic hostelries – with a good choice of real ales and a wide selection of food. All welcome walkers and many have attractions to suit different ages and tastes. Times of opening and when food is served are listed, as well as the telephone number of the inn. Permission has been given for cars to be left at the pubs whilst the walks are undertaken, providing you patronise the inn, but I would ask you to check with the landlord before setting out. Alternative car parking arrangements are also included. If you decide to opt for roadside parking, please be careful not to block any exits or entrances.

In addition, brief details about places of interest within easy driving distance of the walk route are given to help you plan a full day out if you wish.

Should you prefer to use public transport to get to the start of the walks, some of them are within easy reach of a railway station. For times of trains throughout Berkshire, call the 24-hour hot line on 0345 484950.

Finally, I hope you enjoy these gentle waterside walks and will agree that they reflect the best of Berkshire's varied rural scenery.

Nick Channer

PUBLISHER'S NOTE

We hope that you obtain considerable enjoyment from this book; great care has been taken in its preparation. Although at the time of publication all routes followed public rights of way or permitted paths, diversion orders can be made and permissions withdrawn.

We cannot of course be held responsible for such diversion orders and any inaccuracies in the text which result from these or any changes to the routes nor any damage which might result from walkers trespassing on private property. We are anxious though that all details covering the walks are kept up to date and would therefore welcome information from readers which would be relevant to future editions.

EASTBURY AND THE RIVER LAMBOURN

The River Lambourn is particularly pretty at Eastbury, with its little footbridges and swirling plants clearly visible in the swift shallows. The Lambourn rises on the downs near here and flows into the Kennet at Newbury. In winter the river is known to dry up in places. From the village, the walk heads west to neighbouring Lambourn before striding out over the windswept downs on its return to Eastbury.

The Plough, Eastbury.

Eastbury lies in the Valley of the Racehorse, as it has been described by local councils and tourist boards. Generally acknowledged as one of Berkshire's prettiest villages, Eastbury is on the route of the Lambourn Valley Way, a 22-mile walk running through this lovely valley from the market town of Newbury to the Uffington White Horse in Oxfordshire.

During the Middle Ages, the Fitzwarines were lords of the manor here and their splendid old gabled farm with its barns and outbuildings can be seen at one end of the village. The church is mid-19th century and contains a window engraved by Laurence Whistler to celebrate the life of the poet Edward Thomas and his wife Helen who lived at Eastbury towards the end of her life. At the eastern end of the village is the locally famous pigeon house, a charming old octagonal brick and flint building dating from the 17th century and including a spiral staircase and nests for nearly 1,000 birds. The pigeon house was camouflaged during the Second World War, as were a number of other buildings in Eastbury.

The Plough, which lies at the heart of the village, is about 250 years old and is popular with families, walkers and cyclists. Hikers on the Lambourn Valley Way often stop here for refreshment, and various members of the racing fraternity also frequent the inn. John Francombe, thriller writer and former jockey, pops in from time to time. The landlord and his son use fresh produce and bar meals include ploughman's lunches, home-made soup, steak and Guinness pie, stuffed breast of chicken, gammon and scampi. The imaginative à la carte menu offers marinated fillet of lamb, griddled cornfed chicken, fillet of pork, steak and fresh fish. There are always several guest ales on handpump, as well as Dry Blackthorn cider, Guinness, Stella Artois and Carlsberg. The Plough has a beer garden and a safe play area for children. Times of opening are 12 noon to 3 pm and 6 pm to 11 pm from Monday to Saturday. On Sunday the hours are 12 noon to 3 pm and 7 pm to 10.30 pm. Food is served every day except Sunday evening, between 12 noon and 2.30 pm and 6 pm and 9.30 pm. Telephone: 01488 71312.

- **HOW TO GET THERE:** Eastbury is situated a couple of miles south-east of Lambourn. From Hungerford and the M4 (junction 14) take the A338 north to Great Shefford, then follow the signs for Eastbury. From Newbury take the A4 west to Speen and turn right onto the B4000. At the junction with the A338 turn right for Great Shefford and Eastbury.
- **PARKING:** There is a car park at the back of the Plough and limited space elsewhere in Eastbury. Alternatively, park in Lambourn and begin the walk there (point 3).
- **LENGTH OF THE WALK:** 6 miles. Map: OS Landranger 174 Newbury and Wantage (GR 346773).

THE WALK

1. From the inn turn right and walk towards Lambourn for a few steps. Bear right at the footpath sign and head up the track to the route of the Lambourn Valley Way. Turn left here and then left again at the next waymark. Go down alongside the field boundary fence to another waymark; the rear gardens of some bungalows are seen here. Follow the grassy path as it runs beside the gardens, with bushes and fields on the right. At the end of the line of bungalows, continue ahead along the field edge and cross over a track when you reach the field corner. Continue ahead across the next field, following the outline of the path. Pass through a kissing gate, go over a stile and head across a rectangular field. Aim for a line of trees, cross a stile in the next boundary and approach a farm.

2. On reaching a gate in the right boundary, pass into the adjacent field, then bear left and follow the field edge to another stile. Continue on the narrow path between fence and hedge and soon you reach the main Lambourn road. Bear left here and pass Bockhampton Manor Stables. Keep on the road, pass a private drive and then turn right just beyond it to join a signposted byway. Cross the Lambourn and negotiate the next stile on the right. Walk across the field, keeping the river on the right, and make for a stile on the far side. Head for the next stile, then go straight ahead along the road, with the river still close by on the right. Pass some converted barns and then rejoin the Lambourn Valley Way on the right. Follow the path through some rough grass and scrub to reach the sports ground. Make for a kissing gate on the far side by some modern houses. Follow the clear path through the development, passing a timber-framed thatched cottage on the left, and continue to the road. Bear left and pass a fish and chip shop.

3. At the main junction in the centre of Lambourn, turn right into Oxford Street and follow the road to the outskirts of the village, cutting between lines of houses and cottages with a downland ridge visible between them. Bear right into Sheepdrove Road and follow the lane as it climbs quite steeply into the hills. Glancing back on the ascent you can spot the buildings of Lambourn nestling snugly around the church. Pass Highfield House on the left and swing right at the fork just beyond it. Pass Drove Farm on the right and follow the road as it begins to descend, then rises quite steeply between the trees. Note Sheepdrove House on the right, go over a cross track and pass the entrance to

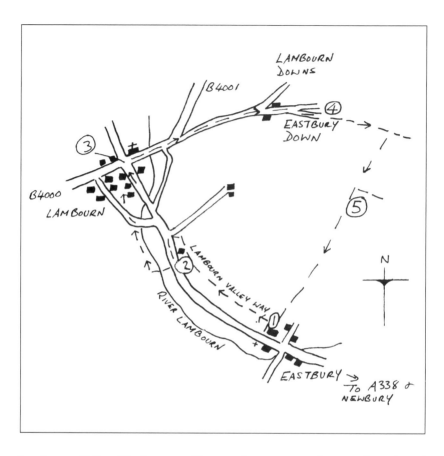

Lambourn Valley Mushrooms. Keep going on a rough, rutted track and veer right at the next fork.

4. Follow the track out over Eastbury Down; the views here are dominated by vast sweeps of remote downland stretching to the horizon. Keep on the track for some time and eventually you reach a junction of rights of way. Bear right here to join a signposted public footpath running along the edge of some trees. There is also a plantation on the right here. Follow the track up the field edge and cross the all-weather training gallops. Continue ahead and make for a gap between trees and hedgerow. Follow the track and when it bends left go straight on towards the steep downland scarp.

5. Cross the all-weather training gallops and then ascend the scarp.

The Downs above Lambourn.

Follow the route of the rough track and gradually a superb view of the Lambourn Valley unfolds before you, stretching away towards Newbury in the east. Continue on the track as it runs between bushes and hedgerows and eventually you reach the outskirts of Eastbury. Pass a corrugated barn, cross the route of the Lambourn Valley Way and head for the road in the centre of the village. The Plough is along on the left.

PLACES OF INTEREST NEARBY

Ashdown House near Lambourn, in the care of the National Trust, dates back to the 17th century and was built as a hunting lodge by the 1st Lord Craven. Tall and ornate, Ashdown is of unusual design, rather reminiscent of a dolls' house. Located on the windswept downs between Lambourn and Ashbury, the grounds and parts of the house are open to the public from April until the end of October, Wednesday and Saturday, 2 pm to 5 pm. Telephone: 01488 72584.

HUNGERFORD: THE KENNET & AVON TOWPATH

Beginning on Hungerford Common, this varied route combines a very pleasant waterside walk with a fascinating town trail. From the centre of Hungerford the route heads for the town's parish church and on to the banks of this historic waterway. Beyond Hungerford Wharf the towpath takes you out of the town for a welcome breath of country air.

The Kennet & Avon Canal at Hungerford.

Hungerford is one of Berkshire's traditional country towns and famous as being a mecca for antique collectors. I lived there at one time and still have fond memories of the place. The broad High Street, which has many antique shops, is lined with Georgian houses and shops, many of which are built in the red and blue brick so familiar to Berkshire. Wide streets are typical of country towns, designed so that markets could be held without blocking the main thoroughfare.

13

Samuel Pepys visited Hungerford in 1668 and ate 'very good troutes, eels and crayfish' at the Bear Hotel, once the haunt of highwaymen.

Completed in 1810, the 87-mile-long Kennet & Avon Canal took 16 years to construct. The final bill was in the region of one million pounds. With 104 locks and many other awesome engineering features, the canal is regarded as a jewel of 18th- and 19th-century engineering. The Kennet & Avon was built to provide a direct trade link between London and Bristol, thus avoiding the treacherous south coast route. The canal eventually became redundant, thanks to the nationalisation of Britain's railway network in the late 1940s. But the Kennet & Avon's dedicated armies of supporters were determined not to let it die. Restored over many years, the canal was eventually reopened by the Queen at Devizes in 1990. The Kennet & Avon and the railway brought prosperity to Hungerford, though the town's golden era began with the turnpiking of the Bath Road in the 18th century.

The Downgate Inn directly overlooks Hungerford Common and is one of the most attractively situated pubs in the area. The inn is thought to date back to the 1700s and was originally much smaller. The front bar, known as the Tool Room and which includes a beamed ceiling and various brass tankards, was extended in the 1970s. Scampi and chips, butcher's style sausages, various ploughman's lunches, jacket potatoes, filled baguettes and toasted sandwiches are among the meals and snacks. The Downgate Inn also offers a children's menu, with fish fingers, turkey dinosaurs and sausage, chips and beans among the dishes. Arkell's 3B features among the real ales, as do Arkell's Summer Ale and Kingsdown. Carling Black Label, Stella Artois, Guinness and Strongbow draught cider are also available. Dogs are permitted. Opening times are from 11 am to 3 pm and 6 pm to 11 pm on Monday to Saturday and 12 noon to 3 pm and 7 pm to 10.30 pm on Sunday. Food is served daily from 12 noon to 2 pm and 7 pm to 9 pm, except Sunday and Monday evenings. On Sunday, apart from a traditional roast, only sandwiches and ploughman's lunches are available.

Telephone: 01488 682708.

- **HOW TO GET THERE:** Hungerford is located 8 miles west of Newbury, just south of junction 14 of the M4. From the A4 by the Bear Hotel, turn into Hungerford High Street. To reach the Downgate Inn turn left into Park Street, just beyond the Three Swans. Follow the road to the cattle grid on the edge of the common and the inn is on the right. There is also a railway station at Hungerford.

- **PARKING:** There is limited parking at the front of the pub, where the walk officially starts. However, there are plenty of parking spaces in the High Street and in Church Street.
- **LENGTH OF THE WALK:** 2½ miles. Map: OS Landranger 174 Newbury and Wantage (GR 343683).

THE WALK

1. From the inn turn left and walk down Park Street, passing the police station which is famous for its colourful hanging baskets. On reaching the High Street, opposite the ornately decorated Victorian town hall, turn right by the Three Swans, cross over by the railway bridge and look for an alley on the left as you approach the Town Bridge.

2. Follow the alleyway into The Croft. With its tree-lined green overlooked by striking houses and villas, this is one of Hungerford's most desirable addresses. Pass the bowls club and on the right is Church Croft Nursery School. Look for an ornate wrought-iron gate and enter the churchyard of St Lawrence's church. The church was rebuilt in the early 19th century after the original building was partly destroyed by, of all things, a heavy fall of snow.

3. Walk through the churchyard to the Kennet & Avon Canal towpath on the far side. Avoid the footbridge leading to Freeman's Marsh and turn right, following the towpath to Hungerford Lock and on to the site of Hungerford Wharf. Russian tallow, the first commercial cargo on the canal, was brought here in 1798. On the right is a row of pretty cottages overlooking the canal. The cottages often appear in various postcards and photographs of Hungerford. Moored narrow boats and motor cruisers are a familiar sight here too. Pass under the Town Bridge and continue on the towpath.

4. Pass under some beech trees and look for a white gate and a bridge with white railings. On the opposite bank is an extensive area of marshes dotted with familiar white willow trees. The next objective is Dun Mill Lock and it is at this point that you leave the Kennet & Avon Canal. Turn left and walk along the road for a short distance in order to appreciate the enchanting view of the Rivers Kennet and Dun.

5. Return to the canal bridge, cross the railway bridge and pass two pillboxes, a Second World War reminder of the threat of enemy

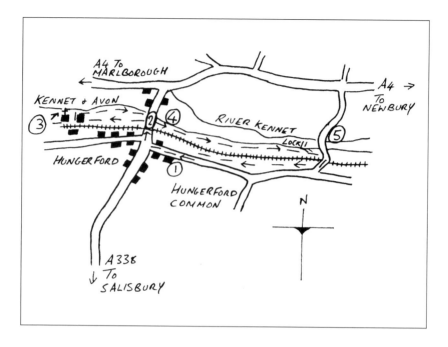

invasion. Turn right at the sign for Lower Denford and Kintbury and cross Hungerford Common. Down to the right, the boundaries of the trout farm at Denford can be seen. Pass some oak and holly trees and head towards the edge of Hungerford. There is no precise path to follow; instead walk ahead over the broad grassy expanse of the common, keeping the valley floor and the Paddington/West Country railway line parallel on the right. The road is on your left. In the 14th century John O'Gaunt, otherwise the Duke of Lancaster, granted fishing and common grazing rights to the residents of the town. His first wife inherited the manor of Hungerford. Continue across the common and back towards the Downgate and Park Street.

PLACES OF INTEREST NEARBY

Walbury Hill is a few miles to the south-east of Hungerford, on the Berkshire/Hampshire border. In May 1944, on the slopes of the hill, members of the 9th Battalion of the Parachute Regiment practised for the first assault into occupied France. The plan was to capture the Merville guns which overlooked the D-Day invasion beaches, and a complete replica of the battery was constructed at Walbury. Nearby is *Combe Gibbet*, a famous local landmark. The views from this high ground are magnificent.

BOXFORD: THE LAMBOURN VALLEY WAY

The scene here is quite delightful in any season, with the River Lambourn winding gently through its lush valley, the soothing sound of water enhancing your enjoyment of the walk. This picturesque ramble begins in Boxford and soon heads for tracts of quiet, pastoral countryside before reaching that riverside stretch of the Lambourn Valley Way.

The River Lambourn at Boxford.

Straddling the banks of the Lambourn, Boxford is one of Berkshire's prettiest villages, with a host of picturesque thatched cottages and fine period houses. At the centre of this community lies Boxford Mill, mentioned in the Domesday Book and now a private house. Opposite is a thatched cottage, once a bakehouse, its garden running down to the water's edge. Note the iron plaque on the bridge, dated 1880. It reads: 'Take notice that this parish bridge is insufficient to carry weights beyond the ordinary traffic of the district and that the owners and persons in charge of locomotive traction engines and other ponderous carriages are warned against attempting the passage of the bridge. By order of the parish surveyors, June 1st 1880.'

The Bell dates back to 1300 and is a traditional country inn and hotel with a strong emphasis on food, all of which is home-made. There are light meals and snacks, including ploughman's lunches, salads and burgers, while the popular bistro menu offers everything from lobster to fillet steak. On Sunday there is a traditional roast. The bar always has four real ales and Tanglefoot and Courage Best are typical examples of what you might find. Lagers tend to be Foster's and Stella Artois. There is Strongbow to suit the cider drinker. The Bell has eleven bedrooms and a beer garden. Well-behaved children and dogs are welcome. The inn is open from 11 am to 3 pm and 6.30 pm to 11 pm during the week and on Saturday. On Sunday the hours are 12 noon until 3 pm and 7 pm until 10.30 pm. Food is served daily from 12 noon to 2 pm (3 pm in summer) and 7 pm to 10 pm. Telephone: 01488 608721.

- **HOW TO GET THERE:** Boxford lies to the north of the A4 between Newbury and Hungerford. Approaching from Newbury, follow the A4 west and at Speen, where there is access to the A34 bypass, join the B4000. Go through Stockcross and turn right at the sign for Boxford. The Bell, where the walk begins, is opposite you at the next junction.
- **PARKING:** There is a room for customers to park at the inn but please tell the landlord if you intend leaving your car here whilst doing the walk. There are also a few spaces elsewhere in the village.
- **LENGTH OF THE WALK:** 3¾ miles. Map: OS Landranger 174 Newbury and Wantage (GR 424714).

THE WALK

1. From the Bell turn left and take the turning signposted 'Winterbourne, Leckhampstead and Chaddleworth'. Go down the lane and pass the route of the former Lambourn Valley Railway which closed in 1959. The line was a vital link for the people of the Lambourn Valley as well as the scattered agricultural and equestrian communities. Though closed for many years, the old line is still recognisable in places. Follow the road round to the left, passing some charming thatched cottages, before reaching a right-hand bend. Avoid the turning to Westbrook and continue through the village. Cross the River Lambourn at the point where it passes under Boxford Mill and note the

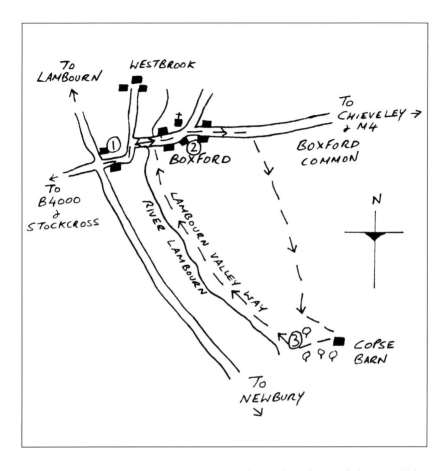

route of the Lambourn Valley Way on the right. The path here will be the return leg of our walk. Keep going through Boxford, veering right at the junction into Winterbourne Road.

2. Pass Tree Cottage and School Lane and make for the crest of the hill. From this point there are good views over rolling fields and woodland. Descend the slope and pass the entrance to Boxford Farm on the left. Turn right just beyond it and follow a signposted public bridleway (Copse Barn). Keep on the track for about 1 mile, making for a bridleway sign on the edge of a wood. Curve left alongside the trees and as you approach some farm outbuildings, turn sharp right to join a waymarked woodland path. Head up through the trees to reach a gate and stile on the edge of the wood. There are glorious views from here over the Lambourn Valley.

19

3. Go straight across the field and drop down to the next hedge line where there is a stile. Bear right to join the route of the Lambourn Valley Way and follow it through the trees. Walk down to the edge of the wood where there is a public footpath sign. A short detour here brings you to the wooded banks of the Lambourn. To continue the main walk, keep right at the junction and skirt the trees, with open fields on the right. Head for a stile and continue ahead with a fence and trees on the left and farmland on the right. Keep to the right of some dilapidated barns, nissen huts and outbuildings and further on the River Lambourn edges into view over on the left, meandering prettily between trees and margins of undergrowth. Follow the riverside path all the way to the road at Boxford, turn left and retrace your steps to the Bell.

PLACES OF INTEREST NEARBY

The ruins of *Donnington Castle*, once an important stronghold, look down over Newbury and the Kennet Valley. The grounds are open to the public. West of Donnington Castle is the pretty village of *Bagnor*, home of the *Watermill Theatre*. The present building is mid-19th century, though there has been a mill here since the time of the Domesday Book. During the 1840s it produced high quality writing paper before becoming a cornmill. In the mid 1960s it was converted into the fine theatre you see today. Over the years the Watermill Theatre has earned much respect from the arts world, with a number of major productions being staged here. Telephone: 01635 46044.

VALLEY VISTAS FROM HAMSTEAD PARK

This charming walk follows the Kennet & Avon Canal as it cuts through some of the prettiest countryside in Berkshire, a landscape of lazy meadows, pleasant wooded hillslopes and fields. Leaving the towpath, the walk cuts across country to Hamstead Park, one of the county's few remaining country estates. From this high ground there are tantalizing glimpses of the Kennet Valley.

The Kennet & Avon Canal.

Hamstead Park is stately English parkland at its best, a classic landscape studded with oak and beech trees and skirted by the River Kennet. Swans, often seen gliding on the water, add a final touch of elegance to the scene. It was Sir William Craven who built a magnificent mansion here in 1660, but the house was destroyed by fire and now all that remains are several sets of crumbling gate piers and some overgrown castle mounds. Said to have been modelled on Heidelberg Castle,

Hamstead Park was designed by the Dutch architect Sir Balthazar Gerbier.

To this day, the Craven family is dogged by tragedy and misfortune. A supposed curse dating back more than 350 years overshadows the family. Apparently, Sir William fathered a child whose mother came from a gypsy family. It is claimed that he refused to marry the girl because of the scandal it would cause. As a result of his rebuff, she cursed the family to the effect that Craven's male descendants would die young. Whether it is the curse or just tragic coincidence, eight male members of the Craven family have not survived beyond the age of 57. Originally Norman, St Mary's occupies a delightful corner of Hamstead Park, its brick tower looking out across the valley. In the corner of the churchyard is a mausoleum containing the Craven family vault.

Marsh Benham is little more than a row of houses between the A4 and the Kennet & Avon Canal. However, it is here that you will find the charmingly named Water Rat, which until the early 1990s was known as the Red House. Before becoming a pub, it was the local village stores and post office and was even a bakery at one time. There are three public areas, consisting of a conservatory and two bars where food is served. It is advisable to book during the week and essential at the weekend. The menu changes daily and the owners also bake their own bread. Smoked haddock and leek tart, roast game patties and steak and kidney pie are typical examples from the lunchtime menu, while supper dishes might include boneless pork chop, home-made pasta and braised shank of lamb. Wadworth 6X and Courage Best feature among the beers on handpump; lagers include Foster's and Kronenbourg. There is also an extensive wine list. Outside is a most attractive enclosed beer garden and terrace with tables and benches. Well-behaved dogs are allowed inside the pub. The Water Rat is open on Monday to Saturday from 11.30 am to 3 pm and 6 pm to 11 pm and from 12 noon to 3 pm and 7 pm to 10.30 pm on Sunday. Orders for food are taken from 12 noon to 2 pm and 7 pm to 9 pm. Telephone: 01635 582017.

- **HOW TO GET THERE:** Marsh Benham lies to the south of the A4 between Newbury and Hungerford. Approaching from Newbury, follow the A4 west, passing a roundabout where there is access to the A34 bypass. Continue for about 1¼ miles and take the second turning on the left to Marsh Benham. Take the first left turning and the inn, where the walk officially starts, is on the right.

- **PARKING:** There is room to park at the pub and permission has been given by the owners for customers to leave a vehicle here whilst undertaking the walk. Alternatively, there is some limited parking near the canal.
- **LENGTH OF THE WALK:** 5 miles. Map: OS Landranger 174 Newbury and Wantage (GR 426674).

THE WALK

1. Turn left out of the inn car park, then bear left towards Hamstead Marshall. Cross the railway line, then follow the road round several bends until you reach the Kennet & Avon Canal. Turn right here and walk along the towpath, heading in a westerly direction. Pass Hamstead Lock and follow the canal as it cuts through a lush landscape of hedgerows, trees and rising hills. Continue to Copse Lock; the River Kennet can be seen over to the right on this stretch of the walk, meandering through the picturesque valley.

2. Pass Dreweats Lock, cross over a weir on the right and continue on the towpath. A pillbox is seen on this section of the walk. Once used as machine-gun posts, these concrete monstrosities were designed to play a key role in the wartime defence of this country. Make for the next bridge which is numbered 73; leave the towpath at this point and cross to the opposite bank. Follow the track diagonally up the hillside and from the top there are lovely, far-reaching views across the Kennet Valley. Follow the track beside barbed wire fencing and along here you are treated to fine views of the ridge of the North Hampshire Downs, defining the horizon. Go through a galvanized gate and as the track curves to the right, veer over to the left to a stile under an oak tree. Once across the stile go diagonally across the field, keeping the escarpment of the downs in view. Head down to a stile leading out to the road.

3. Turn left, pass Old Lane on the right and walk down the road ahead. Pass a gate for Morewood Estate and continue along the lane. Pass a footpath on the right, which runs out across the fields, and head up the slope. Gaps in the hedgerow reveal very good views across the Kennet Valley. The North Hampshire Downs are still in view over to the right. Pass some barns on the left and turn right at the next main junction (signposted 'Hamstead Marshall'). Walk alongside some timber outbuildings and sheds and continue down the lane. Look for a

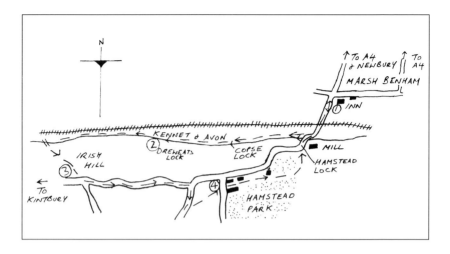

footpath sign on the left after about 150 yards and go through the gap in the hedgerow. Cross several stiles and then head diagonally left across the field, aiming to the left of a large mock-Georgian house. Look for a stile to the right of an electricity transformer and follow the path through undergrowth and vegetation to the road. Cross another stile, go straight over the road and along the drive.

4. Pass Middle Barn, one of a number of converted dwellings on the Craven Estate, and head for two sets of distinctive gate piers. There are impressive views of the Kennet Valley over to the left as you approach them. On the left is St Mary's church. Go through several gates and then follow a grassy track winding through Hamstead Park. The track sweeps round to the left and down through an avenue of trees to join the road. There is a cattle grid here. Turn right by Hamstead Mill, formerly a model mill belonging to the Craven Estate, and retrace your steps back to the inn.

PLACES OF INTEREST NEARBY
Highclere Castle, home of the Earl of Carnarvon, was designed by Sir Charles Barry, architect of the Houses of Parliament, and is the largest mansion in Hampshire. 'Capability' Brown was engaged to create the magnificent parkland for which Highclere, located to the south of Newbury, is so famous. Telephone: 01635 253210.

24

WEST BERKSHIRE'S LAKELAND

If you take the trouble to look beyond Thatcham's modern development you will find pockets of surprisingly peaceful countryside. Among these rural enclaves lies the Thatcham Nature Discovery Centre and it is from here that this delightful walk begins. After a short spell on the road, the route heads south through Thatcham Reed Beds Nature Reserve to reach the towpath of the Kennet & Avon Canal. The circuit is completed on a waterside path along the edge of Thatcham Lake.

Widmead Lock

The site of the Thatcham Nature Discovery Centre reflects a changing landscape, influenced by human activity and the presence of wildlife. The lakes were once part of a series of pits excavated for gravel in the 1970s and they were subsequently reclaimed for wildlife in the 1980s. Today, many of the old flooded gravel pits are used by anglers, and the site is also popular with walkers, who follow the lakeside footpaths, and birdwatchers, many of whom come to seek out the large numbers of wintering wildfowl. The Discovery Centre building was formerly a boathouse built by the then Newbury District Council but never properly used due to restrictions on water activities on the main lake. The Nature Discovery Centre is, in effect, a multi-activity base from which visitors can make their own discoveries. The site includes an interactive exhibition area, study room, artist workshop and refreshment area and is open every day except Monday. For more information telephone: 01635 874381.

Adjacent to the Discovery Centre is Thatcham Reed Beds Local Nature Reserve, which is also an outstanding area for wildlife. Many rare insects can be found here, including the spectacular day flying scarlet tiger moth, and the varied birdlife includes large breeding populations of reed and sedge warblers. Extending to 62.8 hectares, the reed beds at Thatcham represent one of the largest remaining stands of inland beds in southern England. Thatcham village centre, less than 1 mile to the east, offers a good choice of pubs and restaurants.

- **HOW TO GET THERE:** Approaching from Newbury, follow the A4 towards Reading. Continue ahead at the Hambridge Road intersection and take the next turning on the right (Lower Way). The entrance to the centre will be found on the right after nearly 1 mile.
- **PARKING:** There is room to park at the Thatcham Nature Discovery Centre.
- **LENGTH OF THE WALK:** 2½ miles. Map: OS Landranger 174 Newbury and Wantage (GR 506671).

Thatcham Lake

26

THE WALK

1. From the main building follow the track to the road and turn left. Follow Lower Way in a westerly direction towards Newbury. Pass Herons Way and continue to Pound Lane on the right. Bear left about 30 yards beyond it into Prince Hold Road, an unmade road over which runs a public footpath. Pass High Tree Cottage on the right and make for a barrier where there is a sign for 'Thatcham Moors Nature Reserve'.

2. Follow the path alongside reed beds and between margins of vegetation. Veer right at the next bridge and follow the narrow path through the reserve. In a while, the walk passes under the branches of some trees before reaching the towpath of the Kennet & Avon Canal. To the right is Bull's Lock, which was vandalised in the mid 1950s and remained out of commission until rebuilt by canal enthusiasts in 1976. Avoid the lock and swing left by the footbridge to follow the canal in an easterly direction.

3. Pass under the railway bridge and keep going along the towpath. Tracts of unspoilt, pretty countryside can be seen over to the right and the tree-clad upper slopes of the valley signify the northern boundary of Greenham Common. Follow the towpath almost as far as turf-sided

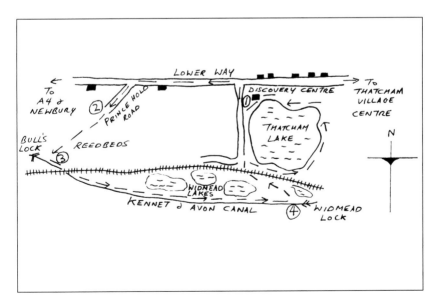

Widmead Lock, which fell into disrepair in the early 1950s as a result of navigation ceasing west of Heale's Lock near Woolhampton.

4. Turn left at a stile and follow the path away from the canal, through a lush, low-lying landscape dotted with lakes and threaded by streams and channels. The walk here cuts between thick margins of foliage and vegetation. On reaching the railway line, cross with care and follow the path down to the edge of Thatcham Lake. Pass through the barrier prohibiting traffic, veer right and follow the edge of the lake round to return to the Discovery Centre.

PLACES OF INTEREST NEARBY

The *Wyld Court Rainforest*, at Hampstead Norreys, on the B4009, east of the village, will appeal to those interested in botany. Here, the distinctive beauty of the rainforest has been recreated under glass. Each of the three houses boasts its own climate and vegetation and there are also various tropical birds, fish, iguanas and small mammals to see. Wyld Court Rainforest is open to the public throughout the year. Telephone: 01635 200221.

BRIMPTON CHURCH AND THE SECRET RIVER ENBORNE

The tall shingle spire at Brimpton church on the upper slopes of the Kennet Valley acts as a useful landmark during this pretty walk, parts of which are beside the delightfully undiscovered River Enborne.

The River Enborne

Most people I know who have done this walk tend to rate it among their favourites and it is easy to see why. It certainly has much to commend it but surely one of its loveliest features is the little River Enborne which flows to the south of the village of Brimpton. Rising on the Hampshire/Berkshire border, to the south of Newbury, this least known of the county's rivers journeys quietly and without fuss through the lush countryside, on its way to meet the Kennet at Woolhampton. The walk begins and ends at Brimpton, which stands on a breezy ridge close to the Hampshire border. A few hundred yards to the south of the church, in the grounds of Manor Farm, lies the Knights Templars' Chapel of St Leonard, founded to help protect pilgrims travelling to the Holy Land. One of Brimpton's great traditions is the annual Pumpkin Day, held in September. Participants are encouraged to cultivate a giant pumpkin which is then dressed for the occasion.

The Three Horseshoes, Brimpton's only pub, dates back to the 1860s and was built as a village local. The lounge bar includes several photographs of the pub – one of them shows the villagers gathered at the front of the building on the occasion of the coronation of George V in 1911. The menu is quite varied with a choice of hot meals and sandwiches. Main courses include rump and gammon steak, ham and egg, curry and rice, battered cod fillets and steak and kidney pie. Jumbo sausage is one of the popular specialities. There is a range of filled jacket potatoes as well as toasted sandwiches and several types of ploughman's lunches. Cheese and chutney, ham salad and prawn salad are examples of the cold sandwiches. Fuller's London Pride and ESB are among the ales drawn on handpump. Lagers include Carlsberg and Kronenbourg; there are also several keg beers. Scrumpy Jack cider is available too. The Three Horseshoes is open from 11 am to 2.30 pm and 6 pm to 11 pm on Monday to Friday. On Saturday the hours are from 11 am to 3 pm and 6 pm to 11 pm and on Sunday from 12 noon to 3 pm and 7 pm to 10.30 pm. Food is served at lunchtime only from 12 noon to 2 pm, but on Sunday the menu is limited to rolls. Well-behaved dogs and children are welcome and there is a pleasant beer garden. Telephone: 01189 712183.

- **HOW TO GET THERE:** From the A4 at Midgham, between Newbury and Reading, head south to Brimpton. Cross the railway and the Kennet & Avon Canal and at the junction in the village centre, turn left. The inn is on the right on a sharp corner.
- **PARKING:** There is room to park at the pub. Alternatively, you can park at the church but preferably not when services are taking place.
- **LENGTH OF THE WALK:** 5 miles. Map: OS Landranger 174 Newbury and Wantage (GR 557646).

THE WALK

1. From the inn turn left and walk along to the village war memorial and seat. Bear left here and head up the drive to the church, located at the end of the ridge. The church dates back to the second half of the 19th century. Take the cinder path to the left of the church and follow

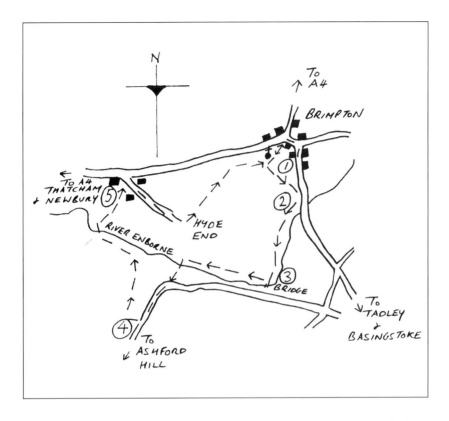

it round the edge of the churchyard. Bear left at some wrought-iron railings and take the track running down the field edge. Ahead of you is a delightful view of the wooded Enborne Valley. Initially, keep a hedgerow and a line of trees on your left, then head down through the fields to the road.

2. At the junction bear right and follow a track. Pass under some power lines and on the right is a good view of the spire of Brimpton church up on the hill. Follow the track; there are trees and bushes and clumps of bracken on the left. Continue until you reach a gap on the left where a footbridge and footpath sign are visible a few yards away. Cross the footbridge, pausing for a moment at this point to admire the trickling little River Enborne drifting lazily, almost unseen, beneath a thick canopy of trees. The path follows a clear line between crops; look for a gap in the hedge on the far side of the field. If the field is ploughed, follow the field edge with the river on your left. The gap is

31

seen just before the corner of the hedge. Follow the path through into a wild meadow bounded by the tree-fringed river. The scene is delightful with a host of wild flowers, long grass and nettles to be seen growing in thick profusion in summer. The sound of the river lapping gently nearby adds to the enjoyment of the walk at this stage. The path skirts the right-hand edge of the meadow, keeping close to a ditch on the right of it. Make for the far corner where there is a stile, with the Enborne close by on the left. The river is narrow and very shallow at this point with water plants streaming just below its surface. On the opposite bank is Inwood Copse, an area of dense woodland. Head across the field and look for a footbridge on the far side.

3. This 45 foot long bridge, spanning the Enborne, was opened in the autumn of 1994. According to one local resident, the original bridge was blown up by a local landowner who claimed that allowing public access interrupted his duck shoot! Don't cross the bridge; instead, turn right and walk upstream, with the river on your immediate left. There is another view of Brimpton church at this point, the distinctive spire peeping above the trees in the distance. Keep going along the riverbank, over a stile and alongside a cream painted house on the right. Follow the river closely and soon you come to a gate and stile. Turn left, cross the Enborne via the footbridge and follow the path through the trees, keeping the river in view until it begins to curve away to the left. Keep to the woodland path, following it to a minor road. Turn right and follow the lane round the left bend. Pass the entrance to a farm on the left and continue through the trees for about 100 yards until you reach a signposted footpath on the right.

4. Follow the field edge alongside trees; further on, the path swings right and passes under some pylon cables. There are pleasant views across gently undulating arable farmland. Make for the field corner, cross a footbridge and swing right. Follow the field perimeter for about 75 yards and take the path leading into the woodland. Pass between trees and margins of undergrowth to reach the edge of an elongated field. Turn left here and skirt the woodland to join a track running along the field edge. The River Enborne reappears on the right. Turn right on reaching a concrete track, cross the river and head up the slope. Looking back, the television mast at Hannington in Hampshire can be seen on the horizon. Pass an oak tree and then head diagonally across the field to the left of it. Make for some woodland on the far side and once through the trees, keep to the right-hand edge of the lawn, passing to the right of the tennis court. Join a grassy path running to the right of a bungalow and follow it between fences.

5. Turn right at the road and follow Hyde End Lane for about ¼ mile. Pass several cottages and turn left at the next signposted footpath. Cut between cottages to a pair of gates and then follow a fenced path running between paddocks. Pass through several more gates and follow the field boundary. The spire of Brimpton church is clearly visible now and over to the right are wide views of the wooded country straddling the Berkshire/Hampshire border. Pass a footpath on the left, running across the field towards the village hall. On the far side of the field you reach a junction with a track. Bear right and walk to the field corner by wrought-iron railings. Brimpton church spire tends to dominate the scene here. At this point, rejoin the path followed at the beginning of this walk and head down to the road. Turn right and walk along the village street to the inn.

Places of Interest Nearby

Watership Down, made famous in the book of the same name, is a few miles to the south-west of Brimpton and is a perfect place for walking. Readers of the classic story will recognise many of the local landmarks and from the summit of Watership Down there are superb views north into West Berkshire.

WALK 7

READING'S HISTORIC WATERWAYS

Reading does not, on the whole, inspire images of unspoilt scenery perfect for a peaceful stroll. However, anyone not that familiar with Berkshire's county town might well be pleasantly surprised by this heritage trail which explores the heart of Reading and takes you along stretches of the Thames and the Kennet & Avon Canal.

The Thames at Caversham Bridge.

Reading is where Jane Austen went to school and Oscar Wilde was imprisoned. The town's industrial heritage is recorded in the local museum and the remains of Reading Abbey, founded in 1121 by King Henry Beauclerc, can still be seen. The Royal Berkshire Hospital, with its distinguished architecture, is also one of the town's gems. Reading is one of those towns that can only be appreciated on foot. A walking tour of its main streets and thoroughfares reveals much of architectural interest.

Built as a private house and now a Fuller's pub, the Fisherman's Cottage, overlooking the Kennet & Avon Canal, is understood to have

34

been an inn for nearly 200 years. It probably became a pub to cater for bargees and others who made their living on the water. From inside, there are good views of all the bustling activity on the canal. The inn's appeal widened with the addition of a light and airy conservatory in the mid-1980s. There is also a pleasant enclosed beer garden. London Pride, ESB and Chiswick Bitter feature among the real ales, while Strongbow Dry cider, Stella Artois, Heineken, Guinness and Carling Black Label are on offer too. Among the dishes found on the menu are pies, deep fried fish, lasagne, chilli con carne, steaks, grills, baguettes, jacket potatoes, ploughman's lunches, various vegetarian meals and a selection of puddings. There is a children's menu and a roast is available on Sunday. The Fisherman's Cottage is open for business from 11 am to 11 pm (12 noon until 10.30 pm on Sunday) between May and October. In winter the hours are 11.30 am until 3 pm and 6 pm until 11 pm from Monday to Thursday and all day on Friday, Saturday and Sunday. Food is available from 12 noon until about 3 pm and 6 pm until about 9.30 pm in summer. Winter times are 12 noon to 2.30 pm and 7 pm to 9 pm though no food is served on Sunday evening in winter. Telephone: 0118 9571553.

- **HOW TO GET THERE:** From Reading town centre, head east along King's Road. At King's Point cross over the junction with the Forbury Road and Watlington Street and continue. On the left is the Prudential building. Turn left into Orts Road and follow it to the far end, then veer left into Canal Way. The Fisherman's Cottage, where the walk begins, is on the left.
- **PARKING:** There is a car park at the rear of the Fisherman's Cottage. Alternative parking is available nearby, or you could park in Reading town centre if you prefer, beginning the walk from there.
- **LENGTH OF THE WALK:** 3½ miles. Map: OS Landranger 175 Reading and Windsor (GR 726735).

THE WALK

1. From the inn turn left, look across the canal to Blakes Lock Museum and after several minutes you pass under a road bridge. Note the colourful murals painted by the people of the Orts Road and Newtown area. The murals depict Huntley & Palmers site and other parts of this corner of Reading. The façade of the Prudential and the remaining building of the old Huntley & Palmers factory can be seen on the right. Continue to the next bridge, with the modern façade of King's Point

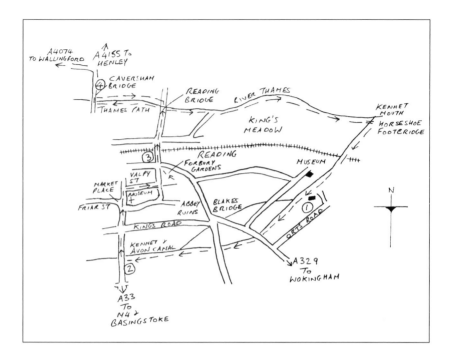

beyond it. Pass Sidmouth Street on the left and the Hogs Head. Continue along the waterfront, avoid a footbridge and follow the sign for the Town Hall and Museum of Reading.

2. Turn right at the next road bridge, go straight over at the next main junction into the Market Place. As the road bends right into The Forbury, aim to the left of St Laurence's church, founded in 1121. The church has a splendid 15th-century tower and the south wall of the nave includes a monument to John Blagrave, a mathematician who died in 1611. Pass the Town Hall and Information Centre on the right, followed by the Museum of Reading and turn right into Valpy Street. Follow the road round to the right into The Forbury and then bear left after about 75 yards into The Forbury Gardens. Pass the lion, erected to commemorate the 19th-century Afghan campaigns, followed by the bandstand and make for the far corner of the gardens, keeping to the left of the Abbey Gateway. Look at the flint walls and abbey ruins, then retrace your steps, heading diagonally across the gardens, keeping to the right of the bandstand. Exit in the far corner, go straight over the roundabout and keep to the right of the Apex Plaza building.

Piper's Island on the Thames.

3. Pass under the railway bridge and cross the next roundabout at the pedestrian lights, following the turning for Caversham and Henley. Head towards Reading Bridge, turning left as you approach it, to join the towpath. Follow the Thames Path along to Caversham Bridge. Cross the bridge, passing the Piper's Island pub on the right, and take the next turning on the right.

4. Follow the riverside path across Christchurch Meadows and recross the Thames at Reading Bridge. Turn left, pass Caversham Lock and then follow the Thames Path alongside King's Meadow. Make for the confluence of the Thames and the Kennet, use the famous listed Horseshoe Bridge to cross the mouth of the river and then follow the Kennet towpath back to the Fisherman's Cottage.

PLACES OF INTEREST NEARBY
Blakes Lock Museum, very close to the route of the walk, includes reconstructions of a printer's workshop, a gentlemen's hairdresser and a bakery. Various aspects of Reading's industrial past are well documented, as well as the history of the town's waterways. Telephone: 0118 9399800.

POTTERING THROUGH THE PANG VALLEY

The River Pang rises on the Berkshire Downs, beginning as an intermittent chalk 'winterbourne' before maturing to a clear trout stream. Swift and shallow, the river snakes through this picturesque valley on its way to meet the Thames at Pangbourne. Beginning in Stanford Dingley, one of Berkshire's loveliest villages, the walk makes for the southern slopes of the Pang Valley before turning north to follow the luxuriant riverbank.

The River Pang

Located on the Pang, Stanford Dingley boasts many fine timber-framed and Georgian houses which stand in the shadow of the 13th-century church of St Denys, famous for its distinctive weatherboarded turret. Few other churches bear the same name and, according to legend, St Denys was martyred in Paris sometime during the 3rd century. Having been beheaded he is said to have picked up his severed head and walked off with it. Medieval paintings depict him holding his head in his hands. It is claimed the church stands on the site of his grave.

Dating back to the 15th century, the Bull is a classic among English country pubs. Inside, there are two bars including the traditional tap room with winter log fire, red quarry floor tiles and barrel chairs. Real ales include Bass and Brakspear and three beers from the locally based West Berkshire Brewery. There is also Strongbow cider, as well as Stella Artois and Heineken for the lager drinker. The main menu contains many appetizing pub meals – cottage pie and savoury pancakes among them. The chef's specials board has a varied and imaginative choice of dishes and changes on a regular basis. There is a small beer garden, and tables and benches at the front. Dogs on a lead please. The Bull is open for business every day except Monday lunchtime, between 12 noon and 3 pm and 7 pm and 11 pm (10.30 pm on Sunday). Food is available from 12 noon to 2.30 pm and 7.30 pm to 10 pm (9 pm on Sunday). Telephone: 0118 9744409.

- **HOW TO GET THERE:** From the A4 at Thatcham, follow the road to Upper Bucklebury. Go across the common and then follow the signs for Stanford Dingley. Turn left just past the Boot, and the Bull, where the walk starts, is on the right, just beyond the bridge. If coming from Reading, follow the A4 to Theale, then head north on the A340. Bear left to Bradfield, then left again at the college. There is a turning on the right to Stanford Dingley and Tutts Clump.
- **PARKING:** There are limited spaces in Stanford Dingley. Alternatively, customers of the Bull can leave their cars there. The landlord has given his consent.
- **LENGTH OF THE WALK:** 3 miles. Map: OS Landranger 174 Newbury and Wantage (GR 577715).

THE WALK

1. From the entrance to the inn, cross the road to the seats and village green. Take the path running alongside the Pang, cross the river and cut between houses and gardens to the road. Turn right, pass the Boot inn and Old Rectory Cottage and continue along the road to a public bridleway. Follow the rough, sometimes muddy track up to a gate and continue in the next field, keeping woodland away to the left. Look for two galvanized gates at a junction of bridleways. Follow the field edge towards woodland, keeping a stand of trees on the right. Make for a stile and galvanized gate and take the path into the wood. Merge with

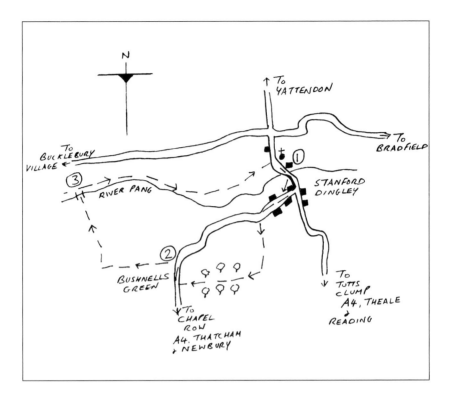

another bridleway and continue through the trees. On reaching the road, turn right and go down to a stile in the left bank.

2. Follow the field edge towards a wooded hillock; there are very good views of the Pang valley on this stretch of the walk. Keep going and eventually you reach the field corner. Bear right and follow the field boundary towards the Pang. Avoid a right of way on the left and keep going on the field perimeter path to reach a gate in the corner. Continue ahead in the next field, keeping the fence on the right, and soon the Pang comes into view. Cross the river by the little footbridge and turn right.

3. Cross a stile and follow the Pang as it meanders through the lush Berkshire countryside. The trees of Bucklebury Common can be seen over to the right, reaching up to meet the horizon. Eventually you come to two stiles. Cross them and take the track down to a gate and footpath sign. Bear left in front of the gate and follow the signposted footpath

Stanford Dingley

(recreational route) diagonally across the field towards trees on the far side. Cross a stile and footbridge and head through the woodland to the next stile. Head obliquely across the field towards Stanford Dingley church and emerge at the road. Turn right and return to the inn in the centre of the village.

PLACES OF INTEREST NEARBY

The Blue Pool at Stanford Dingley, a collection of water from natural springs, is a curious reflective blue. Light is reflected on the particles of mineral glauconite which is present in the chalk. This gives it its blue quality. The pool is well-known in the area and is about 18 feet deep in places. The water is very clear and large trout are known to inhabit it.

THE RIVER PANG AT BRADFIELD

In its middle and lower reaches, strengthened by fresh springs, the River Pang becomes a gravel trout stream meandering through a lush, picturesque valley. This delightful walk follows the Pang through the grounds of historic Bradfield College, revealing in high summer a river dripping with thick foliage.

Bradfield.

It was on the Pang at Bradfield during the 1860s that children played on crude, home-made rafts, punting down to the village from the Old Rectory and then paddling back once more. This stretch of the river is generally acknowledged as one of the loveliest, with charming views of Bradfield College and church from the bank. Just over the bridge is St Andrew's Well which once provided a water supply to the college and the local workhouse. Nearby is a 19th-century gabled brick and flint building, originally the gas works. Close to the church is the mill with a picturesque 18th-century mill house attached. Bradfield College, one of Britain's most famous public schools, was founded by Thomas Stevens, rector of Bradfield, in 1850. Its most famous feature has to be its open air Greek Theatre, buried deep in a disused chalkpit and not easily spotted from the road.

The walk begins at nearby Southend, about a mile to the south-west of Bradfield. Start at the Queen's Head, the only pub in the immediate area and a popular venue for families in the summer months. This is a Fuller's house so the beers tend to be London Pride and Chiswick. For the lager drinker, there is Heineken, Tennent's and Carling. Guinness is also available, as are Strongbow and Scrumpy Jack cider. The menu has a range of starters, snacks and more substantial meals, including sweets. Food is available every day. Main dishes include rump steak, chicken Kiev, scampi and seafood platter. There are also various pies, rice dishes and a choice of two traditional Sunday roasts. The Burger Bar is a popular attraction and offers a selection of filled rolls and other light snacks. The inn, which also serves morning coffee, is open from 12 noon until 2.30 pm on Monday and Wednesday and 12 noon until 3 pm on Tuesday, Thursday and Friday. The evening hours during the week are 5.30 pm until 11 pm. On Saturday the pub is open between 11 am and 3 pm and from 5.30 pm to 11 pm and on Sunday the hours are 12 noon until 3 pm and 7 pm until 10.30 pm. Food is served from 12 noon until 2 pm and 7 pm until 9 pm (snacks until 9.45 pm). Telephone: 0118 9744332.

- **HOW TO GET THERE:** From Theale follow the A340 towards Pangbourne, take the first left turning and bear left at the major junction in the centre of Bradfield. Follow the road into Southend and the pub is on the right.
- **PARKING:** The Queen's Head is the most obvious place to park. Please consult the landlord if you intend doing the walk during opening hours as space is limited. Alternatively park, with care, in the village.
- **LENGTH OF THE WALK:** 4 miles. Maps: OS Landranger 174 Newbury and Wantage and 175 Reading and Windsor (GR – OS map 174 – 596707).

THE WALK

1. From the pub turn left into Cock Lane and pass the surgery and village school. Avoid The Lafford, a residential development, on the right and pass a pair of pretty, timber-framed cottages, also on the right. Bear right immediately beyond them to join a public footpath, following it over a footbridge and between fences and hedges. Make for a stile, then continue along the field edge to a bridleway. Cross over

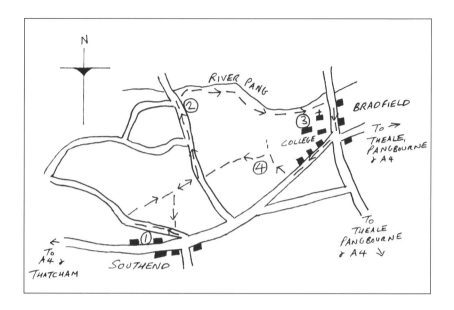

and make for a gate and footbridge. Continue ahead in the next field, passing a large white house on the right, and make for a kissing gate leading out to the road. Turn left and pass turnings on the left for Tutts Clump, Rotten Row and Bradfield Hall Farm.

2. Continue down the lane to a wide gap in the right-hand hedgerow and head diagonally across the field towards some trees. Follow the path alongside the woodland, pass through a gap into the next field and walk beneath the boughs of oak trees. Soon the River Pang edges into view on the left. Follow the path alongside the river; on the right, beyond the fence, are the playing fields of Bradfield College. This reach of the Pang is delightful in any season, with the branches of overhanging trees reaching down to the water's edge. Pass a bridge and continue on the right-hand bank towards the weir and sluice gate. Soon the path veers away from the river to reach Bradfield parish church, restored in 1847.

3. Follow the drive to the road, turn right and pass a telephone box and post box. Bear right at the next main junction and walk beside the buildings of the college. There are pretty views of the Pang Valley between the branches of several oak trees on the right. Continue on the road, taking care on the stretch lacking a pavement. Pass Rectory Lane Cottages and a bus stop and keep on the road as far as the turning for

The Queen's Head, Southend.

the Old Rectory. Turn right here and walk along the drive until you reach a footpath on the left.

4. Go up the slope to a stile and then go straight ahead to a second stile. Continue ahead between laurel bushes, cross another stile and proceed through an avenue of trees. Curve left to a gate, cross the drive to a kissing gate and head straight across the paddock to a second kissing gate in the far boundary. Go straight on, keeping the field boundary fence on the right and making for a gap in the hedge at the top of the field. Beyond it the path forks; keep to the left-hand right of way, following the grassy track to the road. Cross over and retrace your steps across the field and footbridge and on to the next bridleway. Turn left here and go up the slope, following the path through a tunnel of trees. Pass some houses before reaching the road. Bear left and follow Cock Lane back to the inn.

PLACES OF INTEREST NEARBY

Bucklebury Farm Park is several miles west of Southend. The Park is home to many different animals and offers various family attractions. It is open from 10 am to 6 pm every Friday, Saturday and Sunday between Easter and the last Sunday in September. Telephone: 0118 9714002.

BASILDON: TRAILS OF THE RIVERBANK

This stretch of the Thames is especially popular with tourists and walkers as it cuts through some of the finest scenery in the south of England. The famous have known, loved and written about the river, and this part of it is associated with the writer Kenneth Grahame who lived nearby. He wrote 'The Wind in the Willows' in 1908 and found his inspiration for this delightful story here.

The majestic Thames.

The Thames has been used as a highway since early times. Settlements dating back to the Neolithic period have been found on both banks of the river. During the Roman Occupation the Thames was the boundary between the 'civitates' of the Atrebates and the Catuvellauni. The river was probably once navigable to beyond Oxford, although shoals and rapids would have limited its use. In medieval times the Thames was used extensively by barges. An increasing number of weirs for fish traps were built across the river. This was happening before the Norman Conquest, for many mills are mentioned in the Domesday Book. Originally, passage through weirs was via a removable portion called a flash lock. The first pound locks were built in the Jacobean period. Ungoverned weirs caused extensive flooding and various groups of commissioners were appointed to try and regulate the situation, culminating in the setting up of the Thames Conservancy in 1886. Today, the river is administered by the Thames Water Authority and there is a co-ordinated series of weirs and locks controlling the water level and flow of the river.

Lower Basildon has moved away from its original site around the church. The abandonment of the early medieval site is likely to have been caused by frequent flooding. Hence, a move a little further back from the Thames would have been a matter of common sense and convenience. Lower Basildon can be found on the busy A329 Wantage road while Upper Basildon occupies a more peaceful setting on the southern slopes of the Thames Valley. In 1911 Basildon Bond writing paper was named after these settlements when the head of Dickinsons stayed at Basildon Park. Both Upper and Lower Basildon lie close to the Goring Gap where, during the Ice Age, the Thames carved a new passage through the chalk hills and downland.

The Red Lion is a popular inn offering a range of baguettes, a choice of traditional pub meals and various vegetarian options. There are also salads and jacket potatoes. Inside, the pub, which has a friendly, relaxed atmosphere, consists of an extended bar and family area. Among the beers is Tetley; lagers include Carlsberg and Carlsberg Export. Guinness and Dry Blackthorn cider are also available. The Red Lion is open from 11 am to 3 pm and 6 pm to 11 pm on Monday to Saturday, and from 12 noon to 3 pm and 7 pm to 10.30 pm on Sunday. Food is served from 12 noon to 2 pm and 6 pm to 9.30 pm (from 7 pm on Sunday). Telephone: 01491 671234.

- **HOW TO GET THERE:** From Pangbourne, on the A329 between Reading and Goring, take the road beside the church and follow it in a south westerly direction. When it forks, bear right for Upper Basildon. To reach the inn, pass the modern church and at the fork, just beyond it, follow the road signposted 'Ashampstead and Aldworth'. The Red Lion is on the right.
- **PARKING:** The walk is described from the Red Lion and this is the most suitable place for parking. However, you could start in Pangbourne if

you prefer, or even park by the church at Lower Basildon and start the walk at point 4.

- **LENGTH OF THE WALK:** 7 miles. Maps: OS Landranger 174 Newbury and Wantage and 175 Reading and Windsor (GR – OS map 174 – 596761).

THE WALK

1. From the inn turn left and walk up to the village green. Pass Gardeners Lane and follow the road signposted to Pangbourne and Reading. On the left is the modern parish church of St Stephen, built in 1965. Follow the road out of Upper Basildon and after about 1 mile you will see the Old Pump House on the right.

2. Look for a gap in the left-hand boundary just beyond it and walk ahead along the field edge. Make for some oak trees and the remains of a stile in the corner. Pass into the adjoining field and cross it diagonally. There are glimpses here of a fine detached house half hidden behind tall trees. Look for the remains of a kissing gate and go straight on along the field edge, keeping the hedge on the right. Look for a kissing gate in the field corner and make for the trees. Follow the path through a delightful woodland, descending into a sheltered hollow which is particularly attractive in the summer months. Further on, you reach a railway bridge; walk beneath the line to reach the A329.

The Red Lion.

48

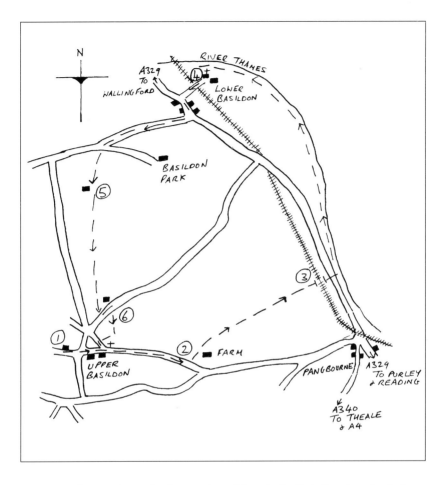

3. Cross the road to a lay-by enclosed by chain link fencing, look for a gate and join the towing path. Keep the river on your immediate right, pass under willow trees and further on the vegetation gives way to meadows and open grassy expanses. The Thames winds its way through a beautiful stretch of the valley, with glorious hanging woods seen over on the Oxfordshire bank. Pass through a gate by some bushes to reach another gate with a galvanized gate beside it. Continue along the towing path until you see the faint outline of a path veering off to the left to a line of trees. Look for a stile and gate here and walk along the field edge to another stile and galvanized gate. Turn left and follow the track along to redundant St Bartholomew's church.

4. The main door is usually locked but a notice advises visitors that there is a key available in Lower Basildon. The churchyard is the final resting place of Jethro Tull who invented the seed drill during the Agricultural Revolution. He died in 1741 and is buried near the main door. Near it also is an elaborate statue in memory of two boys who drowned in the Thames in 1886. Walk away from the church, following the road or the parallel path, and at the main road turn left. Turn right into Park Wall Lane (signposted Upper Basildon) and follow the road alongside the wall for more than half a mile. When the road swings right, go straight on along a bridleway (signposted White Cottage and Redmoor Farm).

5. On reaching the entrance to some corrugated barns and outbuildings, continue ahead to a house distinguished by a verandah at the front. Go straight on along the bridlepath, following it through the woods. Eventually you break cover from the trees to skirt paddocks. Pass under some pylon cables and follow the path as it runs between trees and bushes. Join a track and turn left at the road. Walk along to a handsome Georgian farmhouse and turn right at the footpath opposite.

6. Follow the path as it skirts the field, sweeping to the right in the corner; continue to the next corner and look for the remains of a gate. Pass through a gap in the fence and join a path running between bushes, trees and scrub. On reaching the road, turn left and walk along to the Beehive. Turn right opposite the inn, then right again on the far side of the green. Follow Aldworth Road until you reach the inn where the walk began.

PLACES OF INTEREST NEARBY

Basildon Park is a classical 18th-century house by John Carr. The house, which contains some fine plasterwork, various pictures and furniture, a small formal garden and woodland walks, is open to the public between March and October. Telephone: 0118 9843040. *Beale Park*, near Lower Basildon, is a natural world theme park which includes a deer park, steam railway, willow maze and exotic bird collection. Visitors can also picnic on the grass, stroll by the river, go birdwatching or fishing. Telephone: 0118 9845172.

WALK 11

THE KENNET & AVON CANAL NEAR THEALE

Only by following the towpath of the Kennet & Avon Canal can you fully appreciate the skill and ingenuity applied to the building and design of this renowned waterway. This walk, which demonstrates how the Kennet & Avon has been given a new lease of life in recent years, also highlights the extensive lakes of the Lower Kennet Water Park. Midway round the route, you pass close to the Police Training Centre at Sulhamstead.

The tranquil waters near Theale.

The unusually named Sheffield Bottom, a mile to the south of Theale, is no more than a hamlet, on the road to Burghfield. However, it does boast a pub, the Fox and Hounds, and that is where this delightful walk begins. The inn has been modernised, refurbished and enlarged in recent years and the outcome is a completely new look which suits its many customers. A large restaurant is among the new features. Apart

51

from the faithful locals, there are cyclists, walkers breaking their journey along the Kennet & Avon Canal and ornithologists visiting the nearby lakes.

Wadworth 6X, IPA and Farmer's Glory are among the real ales. Cider drinkers will find Dry Blackthorn on offer, and there is Foster's for the lager drinker. On the menu there are various home-made specials and puddings. Among the starters are soup of the day, melon boat and oriental king prawn platter. Main courses include fillet steak and home-made pies. There are vegetarian dishes, bar snacks, sandwiches, jacket potatoes, baguettes and ploughman's, plus a traditional Sunday roast. Children have their own menu and will enjoy the beer garden and well-equipped play area. The pub is open from 11 am to 3 pm and 5 pm to 11 pm on weekdays. At weekends the hours are 11 am until 3 pm and 6 pm until 11 pm on Saturday and 12 noon until 3 pm and 7 pm until 10.30 pm on Sunday. Food is served from 12 noon to 2 pm and 6 pm to 9.30 pm from Monday to Saturday and between 12.30 pm to 2.30 pm and 7 pm to 9.30 pm on Sunday. There is a restricted menu at Sunday lunch. Telephone: 0118 9302295.

- **HOW TO GET THERE:** Theale lies on the A4, south-west of junction 12 of the M4. Turn south off the bypass (signposted for Theale station) and follow the road round to the right, keeping the railway on the left. At the junction, cross the line and follow the road as it crosses the Kennet & Avon Canal at a set of lights. The inn is further along the road, on the left.
- **PARKING:** There is limited parking in the surrounding roads so it is advisable to park at the inn. Permission has been granted by the landlord.
- **LENGTH OF THE WALK:** 4½ miles. Map: OS Landranger 175 Reading and Windsor (GR 648698).

THE WALK

1. From the Fox and Hounds go out to the road and bear right. Swing right at the junction to join the Theale road. Either side of you are extensive lakes favoured by various species of wildlife. These lakes, part of the Lower Kennet Water Park, were originally gravel pits which dotted this valley. Follow a straight stretch of road for about five minutes, passing the entrance to Burghfield Sailing Club on the right. On reaching a set of traffic lights at the Sheffield Bottom swing bridge over the Kennet & Avon Canal, turn left to join the towpath and follow

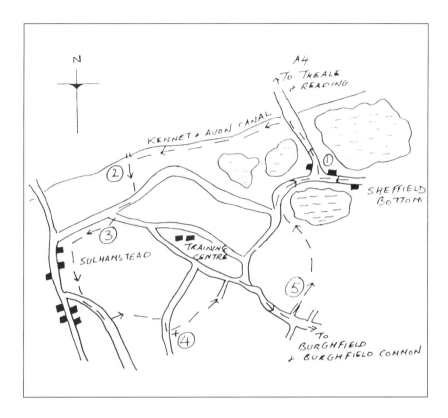

it in a westerly direction. Disregard a footpath to Bottom Lane and continue along the towpath as it runs beneath the branches of some willow trees. Pass a lock and continue beside the canal. At the next bridge turn left to join a signposted path.

2. Keep to the right-hand boundary of the field and on this stretch the outline of the Thames Valley Police Training Centre peeps through the trees on the horizon. Make for a pretty beamed cottage below the trees. Cross a stile and then a wooden footbridge over the river. Follow the left edge of the field to a stile in the corner and make for the road. Turn right here. There are bluebell woods on the left as you follow the lane, and views of the river winding through the fields on the right. When you reach a lodge on the left, bear left for a few yards towards the Police Training Centre and then veer right to join a path along the edge of some woodland. Cross a stile and then bear right, following the white arrow.

3. Note a pretty cottage below the line of the path. In the corner, bear left and then turn right after a few yards into the adjacent field. Bear left and follow the field boundary until you reach a gateway leading out to the road. Turn left and then left again further up at a stile to join a waymarked path. As you cross the stile the distinctive white chimneys of the Police Training Centre become visible. Over to the left across the Kennet Valley is the imposing outline of Englefield House. Follow the path to a stile in the right boundary on the bend of a lane. Cross it and turn right for about 100 yards.

4. Bear left through some gates into the churchyard of a demolished church, veering to the left of a monument recalling the men who lost their lives in the Great War. Pass the remains of the old church – the porch and main door enclosed by stone and flint walls. Cross the stile and make for the next one where there is a path running off to the right. Ignore this path and continue ahead with the field boundary on your immediate left. Join a clear track and after several minutes you reach a private road leading to the Police Training Centre. Bear right and follow it to the public highway. Turn right and walk down the road. The famous water tower at Tilehurst can be seen on the horizon. Follow the road as it twists and turns and then begins to climb. When it levels out, turn left at a signposted path where there is a sign: 'Horsewatch'. Head down the drive and, when it veers right, go left to join a signposted path running out across fields. On the left, in the distance, is an old granary building.

5. Further down, the walk joins a track cutting through an area of pretty woodland. Bluebells are a common sight here in spring. Soon you emerge from the wood at the entrance to the 'Highways Training Centre'. Follow the lane to the road and turn right by a mock Tudor detached house. The road cuts between the lakes as you begin the final leg of the walk. Follow it as it veers round to the right. The lake on the right provides a most attractive rural picture - particularly in spring and summer. At the junction bear right and the pub is on the left almost immediately.

PLACES OF INTEREST NEARBY
The Visitor Centre at *Aldermaston Wharf* offers canal information and sells gifts, souvenirs and refreshments. The towpath here is ideal for a family walk. For more information, telephone 0118 9712868.

FOLLOWING THE FOUDRY BROOK

It may flow unseen in places, screened by a curtain of foliage, but the little Foudry Brook is a classic example of an English stream. Running into the Kennet at Reading, it meanders delightfully through Berkshire's border country. This attractive figure of eight walk follows the stream and explores semi-wooded rural landscapes straddling the boundary with Hampshire.

The Horse and Groom, Mortimer Common.

Mortimer is a sprawling residential village in the south of the county. This part of Berkshire has largely escaped the planner's axe and remains essentially rural and unspoiled. Nearby is The Devil's Highway, a Roman road running from London to Silchester. The road entered Berkshire near Bagshot and then followed a straight course as far as the east gate of the Roman town (Calleva Atrebatum). Mortimer is joined almost imperceptibly with Stratfield Mortimer, its near neighbour, and the prominent spire of St Mary's church at Stratfield Mortimer is clearly seen during the walk. The church contains a Saxon tombstone reputed to be one of the oldest in England and discovered quite by accident when the church was rebuilt in 1869. Hidden behind the church organ is a richly coloured glass mosaic, including a portrait of William of Wykeham of 'manners maketh man' fame and founder of Winchester College.

The Horse and Groom on Mortimer Common offers a good menu – everything from light snacks to substantial meals. Roast lamb, sausage, egg and chips, fisherman's pie and scampi are popular dishes, while baguettes, sandwiches, burgers and soup feature among the lighter fare. There is also a children's menu and a traditional daily roast is served. Real ales include IPA, Wadworth 6X and Marston's Pedigree. Carlsberg Export and Stella Artois are among the lagers. The Horse and Groom has a large beer garden which is very popular in summer. The inn is open from 11.30 am to 3 pm and 5.30 pm to 11 pm on Monday to Thursday and from 11.30 am until 11.30 pm on Friday and Saturday. Sunday hours are 12 noon until 10.30 pm. Food is available from 11.30 am to 2.30 pm and 6 pm to 9.30 pm on Monday to Thursday (no food on Tuesday evening) and all day on Friday, Saturday and Sunday. Telephone: 0118 9332813.

- **HOW TO GET THERE:** Coming from Reading, take the A33 Basingstoke road. Just south of junction 11 of the M4 motorway, turn right, pass through Grazeley and make for Mortimer. There is a railway station at nearby Stratfield Mortimer.
- **PARKING:** There is a public car park opposite the Horse and Groom. The walk begins here.
- **LENGTH OF THE WALK:** 4½ miles. Map: OS Landranger 175 Reading and Windsor (GR 655645).

THE WALK

1. From the village car park turn left and head towards the war memorial. Cross over and take the signposted footpath by the 40 mile per hour speed limit sign at the entrance to Tower House. Walk between the hedge and drive and join an enclosed path between gardens. Soon the path offers far-reaching views across the Berkshire border into Hampshire. Pass between private gardens and fields of crops and walk under the branches of trees before reaching a field corner. Ignore the left-hand turning and strike out across the field, following the path half right to the road.

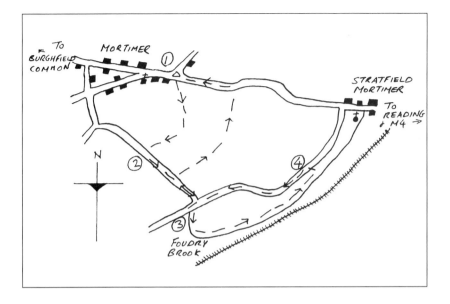

2. Glancing back, there are good views of the houses of Mortimer and Stratfield Mortimer dotted among the trees. Turn left at the road and follow it between trees and hedgerows. Pass a pair of cottages on the left and continue along the lane. Drake House and several cottages are seen on the left. Pass a footpath on the left and continue to the next road junction. Bear right and head down to the footbridge crossing the Foudry Brook. Turn left here and follow the path alongside the water. If you are quiet, you may spot grey wagtails, grey herons or even the blue flash of a kingfisher on this stretch of the walk.

3. Avoid a stile in the field corner and follow the course of the brook as it sweeps left. The church spire at Stratfield Mortimer can just be seen in the distance. Keep the tree-shaded Foudry Brook on your right and continue along the field edge. Cross a stile and make for a second stile at the edge of a field. Turn right and walk along the field perimeter, keeping the brook hard by you on the right. Pass through a gap in the field boundary and a few feet away still is the trickling stream, half hidden in places by the trailing boughs of overhanging trees. On reaching a footbridge, turn left and cross the field, passing alongside several oak trees. Make for a stile in the far boundary and the church spire at Stratfield Mortimer can be clearly seen at this stage of the walk.

Foudry Brook

4. Turn left and walk along the lane, with pleasant views over wooded countryside. Take the first turning on the right and retrace your steps as far as Rosemary Cottage. Bear right at this point and cross the field to a wood. Follow the path through the trees and further on the corner of a field is seen on the left. Keep to the path and pass between trees and margins of undergrowth. Pass alongside a wooden panel fence and join a drive at the entrance to Ashfield. Go up the drive between trees and alongside houses and turn left at the main road. Head back to the centre of Mortimer.

PLACES OF INTEREST NEARBY
Calleva Atrebatum at Silchester near Tadley, to the south-west of Mortimer, provides a fascinating insight into the Roman Occupation when this was the site of an important town. There is also a small museum worth visiting. Telephone the Tourist Information Centre for more information: 0118 9566226. *The Vyne* (NT) at Sherborne St John is about 4 miles north of Basingstoke and is a fine country house which includes a fascinating Tudor chapel with Renaissance glass and a Palladian staircase. Telephone: 01256 881337.

THE RIVER BLACKWATER AND THATCHER'S FORD

The Blackwater is one of Berkshire's lesser-known rivers, flowing serenely along the county's southern boundary with Hampshire. The riverbank provides good views across the Blackwater Valley. This delightful walk begins by skirting Swallowfield Park and then heads south across country to reach the river at Thatcher's Ford, a famous local landmark.

The River Blackwater

Swallowfield lies to the south of Reading in a rural district which was once part of the Windsor Forest. The surrounding countryside is still surprisingly unspoilt and only those prepared to explore it on foot will fully appreciate its varied delights. The 19-mile Blackwater Valley Footpath, a waymarked recreational route runs the entire length of the valley, mostly alongside the river.

The starting point on this circuit is the George and Dragon, located between Swallowfield and neighbouring Farley Hill. Thought to date back several centuries, it has been fully restored in recent years and it is a classic, if remote, country inn boasting a stone flagged floor, low beamed ceiling and part-brick and part-panelled walls, which are adorned with various 18th- and 19th-century sporting prints from *Vanity Fair*. The inn has a good reputation for food in this part of Berkshire, offering a wide variety of dishes from a seasonally changing menu. Ploughman's lunches and sandwiches are among the standard fare; bacon, lettuce and tomato toasted sandwich (BLT) is a perennially popular choice, as is the home-made soup of the day. The George and Dragon is also known for its steaks and fish dishes. Daily specials might include salmon, prawns and scallop salad and bangers and mash in onion gravy. You will find a range of sweets, a traditional Sunday roast, smaller portions of most dishes for children and morning coffee is also served. It is advisable to book a table at weekends. Wadworth 6X and several guest beers are available on handpump, with Guinness, Fosters, Kronenbourg and Dry Blackthorn cider on offer too. Outside is a popular beer garden with tables and benches. Dogs are welcome. The pub is open from 11.30 am to 11 pm on Monday to Friday, from 11.30 am to 3 pm and 6 pm to 11 pm on Saturday and from 12 noon to 3 pm and 7 pm to 10.30 pm on Sunday. Food is served from 12 noon to 2 pm and 6.30 pm to 9.30 pm on Monday to Saturday and from 12 noon to 2.30 pm and 7 pm to 9 pm on Sunday. Telephone: 0118 9884432.

- **HOW TO GET THERE:** From Reading head south on the A33 to cross the M4. Just beyond it bear left and follow the signs for Swallowfield and Farley Hill. Drive through Swallowfield village and head towards Farley Hill. The George and Dragon, where the walk officially starts, is on the left, soon after the entrance to Swallowfield church.
- **PARKING:** There is a small car park at the side of the inn. The walk is described from here and the landlord has consented to cars being parked here whilst the walk is undertaken. However, on very busy days it is easier to park in the vicinity of Swallowfield church.
- **LENGTH OF THE WALK:** 3½ miles. Map: OS Landranger 175 Reading and Windsor (GR 736646).

THE WALK

1. From the inn turn left, then immediately left to follow a path alongside the pub. The grassy path cuts between fields before reaching a waymark. Continue ahead with the boundary fence on your left and

61

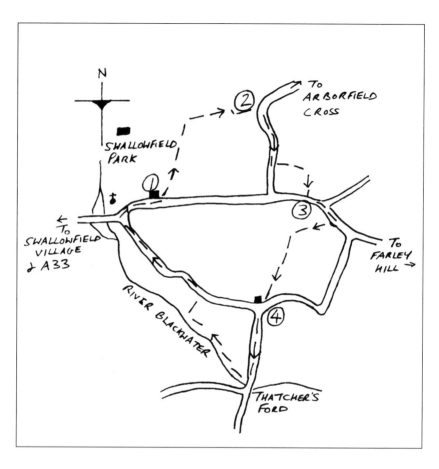

on reaching the next corner, turn right. Pass under the branches of some oak trees and follow the field edge to the next corner. There are several gates here. Go through them to a stile and then follow the parkland track beside oak trees to the road.

2. There are double gates here and an adjoining stile which might be difficult to negotiate during the summer months if overgrown. Turn right and follow the lane between trees and hedgerows until you reach a byway by two sets of wide galvanized gates. Follow the byway, muddy and rough in places, between ditches, vegetation and trees. Pass a public footpath on the left, running into the woods. Curve right, still on the byway, and follow it to the next junction.

3. Cross Priests Hill and turn left (signposted to Farley Hill). Follow the road through the trees for a short distance, turning right to join a signposted public bridleway. Follow the path, muddy in places, between trees and margins of undergrowth. Pass a footpath on the left and walk the edge of a plantation for about 50 yards. Cross a stile and head straight up the field slope, passing between oak trees, and making for the right-hand end of a wood against the top boundary. Cross a double stile into a field and head diagonally across it to another stile. Emerge at the road just beyond it and turn right by a brick cottage.

4. Turn left by a 'ford' sign and go down the lane towards the River Blackwater. Ahead of you now is Thatcher's Ford. The Devil's Highway, a Roman road running from London to nearby Silchester, crosses the river at this point. Take the path on the right just before the ford and follow it alongside the Blackwater. Eventually you reach a galvanized gate; turn right here and cross a stile. Follow the path parallel to some overhead cables and walk along to a stile leading out to the road. Turn left, pass Wheelers Farmhouse and head for the next junction. Bear right and return to the inn.

PLACES OF INTEREST NEARBY
Swallowfield Park, which is owned by the Country Houses Association Ltd, is very close to the route of the walk and is open on Wednesday and Thursday afternoons between May and September. The house is late 17th century and has the Blackwater running through its parkland. Telephone: 0118 9883815. Also nearby is *Wellington Country Park*, which has a wide range of attractions - a lake, a deer park, a miniature steam railway and crazy golf among them. Telephone: 0118 9326444. *Stratfield Saye House*, to the south-west, the other side of the A33, is famous as the country home of the Dukes of Wellington. Telephone: 01256 882882.

EAST BERKSHIRE BORDERS: A LAKESIDE TRAIL

Horseshoe Lake, which covers about 22 acres and is named after its horseshoe-shaped island, lies about ½ mile to the west of Sandhurst. Originally part of an extensive network of working gravel pits that have now been flooded, this restored site occupies an attractive setting in the Blackwater Valley. This very varied walk follows the lake shore before exploring the well-wooded country around Finchampstead Ridges, one of the most delightful areas of Berkshire's borders.

Horseshoe Lake

Finchampstead village is mentioned in the Domesday Book and is one of the oldest settlements in what is left of Windsor Forest. The Forest officially disappeared in 1817 when the Crown received 6,665 acres as compensation for the surrender of a variety of rights.

There is plenty of scope for a stroll beside Horseshoe Lake. A bridleway runs along the northern boundary and a clear path circumnavigates the lake, providing very pleasant views of the site and the surrounding countryside. Horseshoe Lake is now established as an extremely popular venue for those who enjoy dinghy sailing, windsurfing, canoeing, birdwatching and walking.

The Greyhound is a popular family pub with a good choice of food and drink. Meals include steaks, half a roast chicken, traditional fish and chips, breaded plaice and a selection of vegetarian dishes. There are usually up to six daily specials too. Light snacks tend to feature sandwiches and a choice of baps. Home-made soup is on offer and, on Sunday, a range of traditional roasts. A children's menu is available. Real ales include Fuller's London Pride and Wadworth 6X, while Heineken Export and Stella Artois are among the lagers. Outside is a beer garden with a play area for children. The Greyhound is open between 11 am and 11 pm from Monday to Saturday and between 12 noon and 10.30 pm on Sunday. Food is served from 11.30 am to 10 pm (12 noon until 10 pm on Sunday). Large groups of walkers are welcome but are requested to book. Telephone: 0118 9732305.

- **HOW TO GET THERE:** Finchampstead is located on the B3348, between the A321 and the A327, about 7 miles south of Reading. The Greyhound, where the walk begins, lies in the centre of the village.
- **PARKING:** Ideally, park at the Greyhound; the landlord is agreeable for walking customers to park here and there is a spacious car park. Alternatively, there is a car park by the Blackwater Valley Footpath at point 2 of the walk.
- **LENGTH OF THE WALK:** 5 miles. Map: OS Landranger 175 Reading and Windsor (GR 795631).

THE WALK

1. On leaving the pub, turn right and go down the road to the junction with Longwater Lane. Bear left here into Cricket Hill and follow the lane alongside a row of houses, cottages and bungalows. Fields and trees make up the picture on the left. Follow the road as it swings left into Lower Sandhurst Road and keep going as it cuts through a rural landscape of low-lying fields and light woodland. The River Blackwater, symbolizing the boundary between Berkshire and Hampshire, lies over to the right. Pass Dell Road on the left and continue to Blackwater View, a private road on the left.

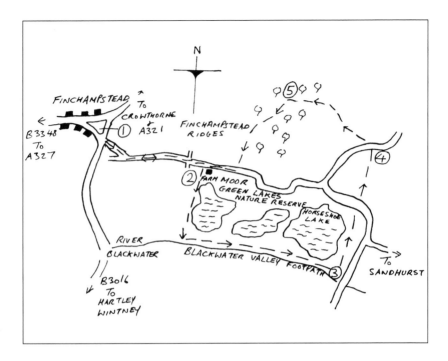

2. Turn right here and pause for a few moments to admire the view of the Blackwater Valley. This part of the valley includes Moor Green Lakes Nature Reserve, an important habitat for breeding and wintering birds. The reserve was once part of a sand and gravel quarrying operation. Follow the waymarked Blackwater Valley Footpath, cross over a stream and continue on the path, muddy in places, between fences and hedges. Eventually the path turns sharp left; follow the path between lakes on the left and the River Blackwater on the right. Do not cross the footbridge ahead; instead keep to the Blackwater Valley Footpath. On reaching a kissing gate and a sign for 'Horseshoe Lake', turn right and follow the riverbank.

3. As you approach a road, swing left through a gate and follow the path along a section of boardwalk, which is often slippery in wet weather. Keep to the Blackwater Valley Footpath, veer left and head towards the Horseshoe Lake Watersports Centre. Go straight on along a waymarked path and continue to the lake corner. Pass through a kissing gate, step over a muddy bridleway to a second kissing gate and head out to the road. Cross over to a third kissing gate and skirt the field by

66

The Greyhound pub

keeping close to the left-hand hedge and fence. Negotiate a stile in the corner and make for some trees ahead. Pass through another kissing gate and then turn left at the road.

4. Walk along to a sign for 'Bluebells Farm'. Turn right here and follow the drive through the trees. When it bends left, go straight on along a path cutting between fence and woodland. The path eventually curves left, with fields and woodland seen either side of you. Follow the path through the trees and veer right at the fork. Take the sunken path up through the woodland and undergrowth; continue ahead on the higher ground, following the path through extensive woods. A wooded dell can be seen on the left. Keep right here and right again at the next fork. On reaching a bridletrack, turn left.

5. Follow the track as it descends through the trees. Banks of bracken and undergrowth can be seen on this stretch of the walk. Pass several houses and various paddocks and in the distance you can spot the Blackwater Valley, away to the south. Pass a turning on the right for Finchampstead Ridges where the National Trust owns 60 acres of lovely woodland, including a heather ridge. There is an extensive network of paths and much to interest the naturalist and ornithologist.

Spotted flycatchers and siskins are among the many species to be found here. If time allows, you may like to deviate from the route of the walk at this point and wander down to a pond, or perhaps continue beyond it to admire the attractive scenery. Returning to the main walk, keep on the track down through the trees, passing a property called 'Old Thatch' with a thatched gate at its entrance. Continue down to Moor Green House and turn right at the road. Pass Foxglade Farm and return to the centre of Finchampstead.

PLACES OF INTEREST NEARBY

California Country Park, north of Finchampstead, is a popular attraction with families. The park includes many different species of trees, a lake, a dragonfly pond, fishing, children's play equipment and an information centre. Telephone: 0118 9730028. *The Look Out Discovery Park*, at Nine Mile Ride, south of Bracknell, is situated in 2,600 acres of woodland. There are walks and nature trails, a gift shop, picnic area, tourist information centre, coffee shop, children's events and exhibitions. The site also has plenty of free car parking. Telephone: 01344 868222.

A WALK AT VIRGINIA WATER

One of the great attractions of Windsor Great Park is Virginia Water, a large ornamental lake fringed by trees. Paths and rides circumnavigate the lake, and this glorious walk, perfectly reflecting the changing seasons, never strays far from the water's edge, providing constant views across Virginia Water to its wooded fringes.

Virginia Water

Virginia Water covers about 160 acres, is a little over 2 miles in length and straddles the Berkshire/Surrey border. The lake was developed in the middle of the 18th century for the Duke of Cumberland after his victory at Culloden. Before the lake was created, the land was part of a swamp. George IV ordered that a scaled down frigate be built for the lake, which was still in existence during the reign of Queen Victoria. Virginia Water lies firmly within the boundaries of Windsor Great Park which stretches south from Windsor Castle to Chobham Common in Surrey. Comprising about 4,800 acres of wooded parkland and gardens, the design and landscaping of the park were largely carried out by the Duke of Cumberland.

The Wheatsheaf, on the A30 near Virginia Water, is a classic example of an old roadhouse – a large inn or restaurant on a main road in a country area. Recently refurbished, it is now a Chef and Brewer pub and restaurant. The menu ranges from light snacks such as jacket potatoes and sandwiches to more substantial fare like steak and kidney pudding and spinach and red pepper en croute. It is open Monday to Saturday 11 am to 11 pm (Sunday hours 12 noon to 10.30 pm) and serves food all day. The Wheatsheaf is also a hotel offering accommodation and there is a tearoom in its conservatory where morning coffee, light lunches and afternoon teas are available. The tearoom is open April to September from 9 am to 6 pm or dusk, whichever is earliest, and October to March from 10 am to 5 pm, or dusk. Telephone: 01344 842057.

- **HOW TO GET THERE:** Virginia Water lies east of Bracknell, close to where the A329 joins the A30. From Windsor head south through Englefield Green to join the A30. Turn right just beyond the Wheatsheaf, following the A329 to the Blacknest car park entrance which is on the right.
- **PARKING:** There is ample room to park at the Blacknest car park. If you prefer, park off the A30, at the eastern end of the lake, where there is also plenty of room and start the walk at point 4.
- **LENGTH OF THE WALK:** 4 miles. Map: OS Landranger 175 Reading and Windsor (GR 961686).

THE WALK

1. From the Blacknest car park go through the gate and look for a sign for Frost Farm Plantation. The woodland here is composed mainly of large and old oak, beech, sweet chestnut and hornbeam. Dead and decaying timber associated with the mature trees provides a habitat for many rare toadstools and insects – especially beetles and flies. Nuthatches, tree creepers, woodpeckers and the exotic mandarin ducks, often seen on the lake, also inhabit the forest. The area is managed by the Crown Estate. With the gate behind you go straight ahead along the sandy path; Virginia Water can be seen in the distance. As you approach the water, veer off to the left and the graceful outline of the classical bridge can be seen framed by trees. Follow the hard lakeside ride and turn right at the head of the lake; look for a sign 'horses and cycling prohibited'. Soon the path merges with a metalled road; follow it to the bridge and then continue ahead along a path running parallel to the road. Pass entrances to some houses and keep ahead on the grassy path. Head along a causeway, keeping trees on the right and water either side of you, and once across it bear right by some railings.

2. Follow the path alongside the northern arm of Virginia Water. A house with gardens sloping down to the water's edge can be seen over to the right. The main body of Virginia Water can be seen ahead, ringed by woodland. Keep to the path and pass various signs for 'Valley Gardens'. This spectacular shrub garden, open to the public, covers 450 acres and was begun in 1935. There are also good views of Virginia Water between clumps of beech trees on this stretch of the walk. Continue beside ornamental species, cedar trees and lines of rhododendron bushes. Eventually the path curves away from the lake and cuts between trees and grassy clearings. Common beech and common oak are among the species that have been replanted in this part of Windsor Great Park. Hornbeam, lime and cherry are also included. The new planting replaces the beech and oak which were originally planted about 1750 and blew down in the gales of 1987 and 1990. Veer left at the fork and, on reaching the Totem Pole, bear right at the sign for 'Virginia Water car park and Wheatsheaf Hotel'.

3. Commemorating the centenary of British Columbia in 1958, the Totem Pole is 100 ft high – a foot for every year. It was presented to Her Majesty the Queen during her visit there. The totem pole is a characteristic feature of Pacific coast Indian art and this particular one is carved from a log of western red cedar which is native to the west coast of Canada. Keep the lake on the right now, as you follow the path south. To visit the Wheatsheaf Hotel, walk through the car park on the left, go out to the A30 and turn right for a short distance. The Wheatsheaf is on the right.

4. Return to the lakeside path and continue south until you reach a triangular junction with some trees in the middle. There is also a sign prohibiting paddling and bathing. Leave the lakeside path and follow the metalled road down towards the A30. Keep to it as it swings right and heads down between the trees to a bridge over the Virginia Stream. Cross over and look up to see the artificial dam with the water cascading down over the rocks. Go up the slope and further up, when you break cover from the trees, there is a splendid view of the lake. In

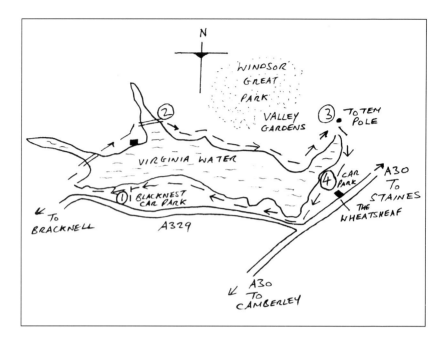

wet weather, an air of mystery seems to descend over these surroundings, with the mist enveloping Virginia Water and its tree-lined banks. On the left on this stretch are the remains of a colonnade of ancient stone pillars erected in 1827 as a landscape feature at the behest of King George IV, having been imported in 1818 from the Roman city of Leptis Magna in Libya. Keep going until you see the classical bridge edging into view across the lake. Look for a path running off half left through the trees and follow it back to the car park at Blacknest.

PLACES OF INTEREST NEARBY
The Savill Garden, to the north of Virginia Water, comprises 35 acres of unspoilt woodland, azaleas, magnolias, rhododendrons and herbaceous borders seen at their best during summer. There is also an extensive display of roses. The garden, which was started in 1932 by Sir Eric Savill, Deputy Ranger of Windsor Great Park, also includes a gift shop, self-service restaurant and Temperate House. Telephone: 01753 860222. *Windsor Castle* was founded as a fortress by William the Conqueror over 900 years ago. A tour of the castle includes the Precincts, State Apartments and St George's Chapel. Telephone: 01753 831118.

THE THAMES AND THE PLAYING FIELDS OF ETON

The riverside at Datchet has always been popular with visitors and locals, and the scene is enhanced by its views of Windsor Castle, Home Park and the Thames downstream. The walk begins in the village and soon heads for the playing fields of Eton where, according to Wellington, the Battle of Waterloo was won. Beyond the cloisters and the quadrangles of Eton College, the path makes for riverside meadows before crossing historic Windsor Bridge. The return leg is along the opposite bank of the stately river as far as Home Park. The splendid battlements of Windsor Castle and its majestic Round Tower are constantly within sight along the route.

The Thames looking towards Windsor Castle.

Datchet has several strong literary associations. The main road to Windsor, at the southern end of the High Street, was the Datchet Lane in Shakespeare's *The Merry Wives of Windsor*. Falstaff was transported along this road on his way to face the ordeal of a ducking in the Thames. The village is also mentioned in Jerome K. Jerome's *Three Men in a Boat*. One mile above the village, accompanied by the Provost of Eton College, the legendary angler Izaak Walton used to fish 'for a little samlet or skegger trout, and catch 20 or 40 of them at a standing.' Just before the turn of the century, and again soon after the Second World War, Datchet suffered serious flooding when the swollen Thames caused a pond in the centre of the village to overflow. Several anxious residents were isolated in their homes.

The Royal Stag, overlooking The Green at Datchet, was once the home of Robert Barker, printer to Elizabeth I. The menu caters for most tastes and snacks include filled baguettes, soup of the day and jacket potatoes. More substantial dishes range from scampi and mixed grill to lasagne and steak and kidney pie. There is also a Sunday roast, as well as a specials board. Beers include Burton, Marston's Pedigree and Tetley, and there is a guest ale which changes fortnightly. Castlemaine XXXX and Stella Artois are among the lagers, and there is Dry Blackthorn cider. The inn is open from 11 am to 11 pm on Monday to Saturday and between 12 noon and 10.30 pm on Sunday. Food is available every day except Sunday evening, and is served from 12 noon to 2 pm and 6 pm to 8.45 pm. Telephone: 01753 548218.

- **HOW TO GET THERE:** From the M4 head south to Datchet (junction 5 or 6). The walk begins at The Green which is just to the north of the railway line.
- **PARKING:** Use the station car park at Datchet if there are spaces. Alternatively, park elsewhere in the village, or leave your car in neighbouring Windsor and start the walk at point 5.
- **LENGTH OF THE WALK:** 5½ miles. Map: OS Landranger 175 Reading and Windsor (GR 987771).

THE WALK

1. From The Green in the centre of Datchet head south along Datchet High Street towards the Thames, crossing the railway line. Continue to the junction and opposite are seats under the trees, allowing you to pause here and enjoy the tranquil scene. Walk along the B470 road, keeping the Thames on the left, pass Queens Road and take the path on the right immediately beyond a house called 'Sumpter Mead'. Follow the path through the spinney and emerge from the trees on the edge of a golf course. Proceed ahead along the edge of the fairways, keeping trees and hedgerow close by on the left. Further on, there are teasing glimpses between the trees of the Thames and the graceful outline of Windsor Castle on the horizon. Continue to a green at the far corner of the course and join a path between fences. Veer left at the fork, pass beneath the railway line and go through a kissing gate.

2. Cross the paddock, aiming towards a stile. Immediately ahead of you is the slipway of Eton College Boathouse sloping down to the river. Proceed over the slipway to the road and continue ahead, soon joining a path running parallel to the pavement. Note the path on the opposite side of the road, running through an avenue of trees. The path leads to neighbouring Slough. Cross over a stream and follow the path through parkland belonging to Eton College. As you approach a bridge over a stream known as The Jordan, swing sharp right and then bear left after several yards, following the path as it curves round towards the cricket pavilion. Pass through a kissing gate and turn left along the B3022. As you cross the road bridge towards Eton and Windsor, there is an unforgettable view of Eton College Chapel, with Windsor Castle standing proudly above the river. The college was founded in 1440 by Henry VI who was aged just 19 at the time. Modelled on Winchester College, Eton is the second oldest public school in the country. The boys still wear black tail coats in mourning for George III, their favourite monarch. On reaching the entrance to Eton College, turn right by the School Library into Common Lane and on the corner here is an ornate Victorian lamppost known as the Burning Bush.

3. Veer left after a few yards and then take the path, known as Judy's Passage, to the right of Holland House. When you reach the end of the path, turn left for several yards and then swing right to join a signposted path. Follow the path between a wooden fence and a brick wall towards a field distantly visible at the end. On reaching the field, veer left and after a few yards you reach the road. Cross over and follow the tarmac path with allotments and the arches of a seemingly endless railway viaduct on your right. Turn right at the next footpath sign, pass through one of the arches of the viaduct. Confusingly, Windsor and Eton, only a matter of yards apart, are served by different railway lines. This viaduct carries Brunel's Great Western Railway above the flood plain on the Windsor to Slough line. Once through the arch veer half left across the field towards a smattering of trees beside the Windsor bypass. As you cross this field there is a wonderful view of Windsor

The Royal Stag, Datchet.

Castle over on the easterly horizon. The castle was founded as a fortress by William the Conqueror and has been substantially altered and extended over the centuries. The most recent work undertaken followed the much publicised fire in 1992. On reaching a narrow lane running beneath a canopy of trees, turn left and after a few yards, at the end of the fence on the right, bear right and right again at the fork. Keep the woodland on the right and along this stretch another splendid vista reveals Windsor Castle rising above the railway viaduct. Soon you arrive at the riverbank; turn left and follow the Thames Path.

4. Pass under the railway bridge and follow the riverside path onto The Brocas, an extensive area of broad open commonland belonging to Eton College. From here there are unbroken views of Windsor Castle in front of you, with the houses of Eton and the College Chapel over to the left; the opposite bank of the river is draped in overhanging willows. It is an enchanting scene and a once popular haunt of the artist, Turner. Swing slightly away from the river and make for the exit; pass the Waterman's Arms and soon you reach the junction with Eton High Street. If time permits, you may wish to amble among the shops and quaint old buildings here. Return to this point, cross Windsor Bridge

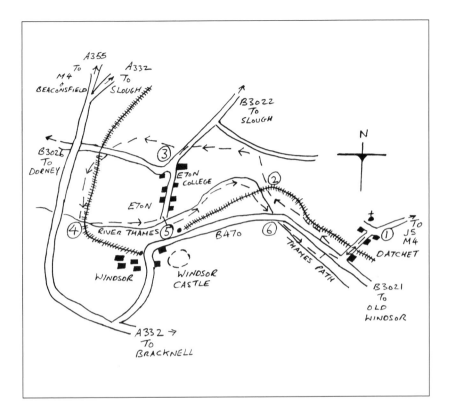

and then bear immediately left down the steps towards the Donkey House pub overlooking the river.

5. When you draw level with the inn, pass through a set of wrought-iron gates and follow Romney Walk. To the right are the car park and buildings of Windsor and Eton Riverside Station. The Royal Waiting Room was built in 1849. There are good views up to the castle, as well as glimpses of Eton College Chapel through the trees beyond Romney Island. Continue ahead on a drive, pass a cottage dated 1898 and a distinctive octagonal building which houses the waterworks for Windsor Castle. On reaching a boatyard, look for a kissing gate by the boat hoist and close to the riverbank. Walk along the grass towpath beside the river; Eton College Boathouse is soon visible on the opposite bank. Pass under the 19th-century Black Potts railway bridge and skirt the playing fields on the right. As you approach the next bridge, veer right to the Thames Path sign at the far end of the white railings, turn

The Thames at Windsor.

left and follow the pavement over Victoria Bridge, built in the mid-19th century and partly designed by Prince Albert. Over to the right is Home Park – 4,000 acres of private land belonging to Windsor Castle.

6. Turn right to join the Thames Path, following it through the trees with delightful views of the Thames and Home Park beyond. On reaching the road, turn right along the B470 and then bear left into Datchet High Street. Retrace your steps to the centre of the village.

PLACES OF INTEREST NEARBY
Legoland, to the south of Windsor is set in 150 acres of magnificently landscaped parkland, with wonderful views over Windsor and its castle. At Legoland visitors can explore a castle filled with dragons and woods teeming with pirates. There are driving schools for children and European landmarks made from millions of Lego bricks. For more information, or to book in advance, telephone: 0990 040404.

THE THAMES AT COOKHAM

This stretch of the Thames, between Maidenhead and Marlow, is one of the loveliest and certainly one of the most famous. Photographs taken at the end of the 19th century and during the 1920s illustrate the riverbank's potential for picnicking, with many families relaxing by the water's edge. Beginning at Cookham, the walk follows a lengthy stretch of the Thames Path before heading towards Winter Hill, a dramatic viewpoint overlooking the valley and the distant Chilterns. From here it is a pleasant stroll over Winter Hill golf course and back to Cookham.

Cookham.

The controversial artist Stanley Spencer made his home in the picturesque Thames-side village of Cookham and lived here until his death in 1959. The Spencer Art Gallery, formerly a Nonconformist chapel, is where his highly individual style is perfectly illustrated. Officially opened in 1962, the gallery exhibits many of Spencer's paintings, including *The Last Supper*. An eccentric figure, Spencer was often seen pottering about the village, pushing a pram which contained his paints and easel. A tour of Cookham's streets provides no clues that the Thames is only a matter of yards away, but a short walk through the churchyard of Holy Trinity brings you to a delightful reach of the river.

The Kings Arms, once a hotel, is one of Cookham's most famous inns and offers a wide-ranging menu. Soup of the day is perhaps an obvious choice if you have been out walking on a crisp winter's morning. There is also a range of sandwiches and the classic bacon, lettuce and tomato sandwich, otherwise known as BLT. Among the specials are beef stew, burgers and fish and chips. The restaurant offers a good choice of dishes, including a traditional Sunday roast and several vegetarian options. Boddingtons features among the range of beers, and the lagers include Stella Artois and Heineken. The cider is Strongbow. Outside there is a popular beer garden, a large car park and a play area for children. The Kings Arms is open between 11 am and 11 pm on Monday to Saturday and from 12 noon until 10.30 pm on Sunday. Food is served from 12 noon until 2.30 pm and between 5 pm and 10.30 pm on weekdays and Saturdays, and from 12 noon until 10.30 pm on Sunday. Telephone: 01628 530667.

- **HOW TO GET THERE:** Cookham lies several miles north of Maidenhead on the A4094. Turn off westwards into the High Street (B4447).
- **PARKING:** The most suitable place to leave a car is the car park on Cookham Moor, off the B4447 at the western end of the village. Cookham has a good choice of pubs and restaurants which are all within easy walking distance of the car park.
- **LENGTH OF THE WALK:** 4½ miles. Map: OS Landranger 175 Reading and Windsor (GR 894854).

THE WALK

1. From the car park on Cookham Moor, where stray animals were once kept, turn left and walk along to Cookham High Street. Pass the Kings Arms and on reaching the next main junction you can see the Spencer Gallery on the right-hand corner. Turn left and walk along the A4094 for a short distance. Over on the right is the Tarry Stone, a sarsen boulder which has occupied different positions over the years. Games were played around it on Assumption Day until the 16th century. During the 19th century it sat in a private garden until it was recovered by the people of Cookham and transferred to its present setting in 1905.

2. Bear left for Holy Trinity church, noting its imposing 15th-century tower, and follow a path running to the left of it, heading for a wrought iron kissing gate on the far side of the churchyard. Join the Thames Path at this point and head upstream away from Cookham Bridge. Built in 1867, it came to be known as 'the cheapest bridge across the Thames' and there was a toll in operation until the late 1940s. Go through several gates before reaching Bourne End railway bridge. Originally a simple wooden structure carrying a single track, the present single track iron and steel bridge was opened in 1894. At one time it was agreed that the bridge should be widened to allow a second track in the days when the line ran to High Wycombe. This never happened and today the bridge is reduced in status, forming part of the Maidenhead, Bourne End, Marlow shuttle service.

3. Pass rows of chalets and bungalows to reach Cock Marsh. Now in the care of the National Trust, the marsh includes four bowl barrows or prehistoric burial mounds, the largest of which has a 90 foot circumference. When excavated in the 19th century it was found that two of the barrows contained early Bronze Age burials dating back 4,000 years. Continue along the riverside path and you will see the steep chalk escarpment of Winter Hill in the distance. Keep to the left of Ferry Cottage and now the walk's surroundings become increasingly more isolated as you head towards the bulk of the hill. As you approach a concrete drive, turn left across a field and make for a kissing gate in the far boundary. Go forward to a signpost, bear right and head diagonally up the grassy slopes of Winter Hill.There are stunning views across the Thames Valley at this stage of the route. Head up to a gate and join the road opposite the entrance to a house called 'Chimneys'.

4. Turn left and follow the road to a fork. Keep left here for Cookham, following Terry's Lane. Walk along the road, turning left immediately before the entrance to September Grange. Follow the right-hand edge of the field to its corner where there is a junction of paths. Turn right and pass a sign: 'Footpaths cross golf course'. Keep a wooden panel fence, wire fence and hedge on the right and descend the hill slope towards the valley. Head down over the windswept fairways and aim to the left of some corrugated barns. Make for the footbridge over the railway line in the distance.

5. Once across it bear right and initially keep the embankment hard by

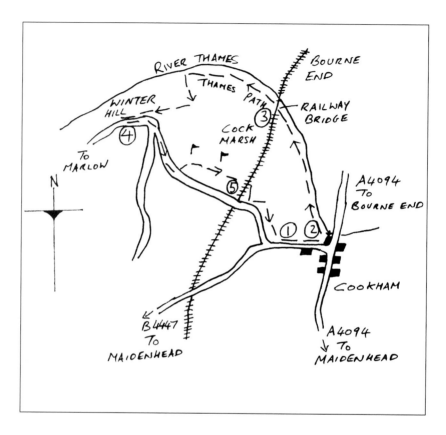

you on the right. Further on, join a stony track and turn left beside the entrance to a house called 'Fiveways'. Follow the path between a hedge and fence and soon you reach a kissing gate. Bear right towards Cookham Moor, pass through a kissing gate and cross a footbridge into the car park where the walk began.

PLACES OF INTEREST NEARBY

Maidenhead has plenty of things to see and do. A visit to Boulter's Lock is recommended. During the Edwardian era, this most famous of landmarks was a particularly fashionable spot on the river, with the scene brought to life by a colourful parade of punts and parasols. Large crowds came here in search of peaceful recreation and this part of the town remains just as popular today. A boulter was another name for a miller. For more information about Maidenhead contact the tourist information centre on 01628 781110.

HURLEY: THE THAMES PATH

This walk saves the best until last. On reaching the Thames you cross the river to a small island where you can admire all the bustling boating activity. The last mile follows a glorious stretch of the Thames, with cattle often seen grazing by the water's edge, a timeless picture at any time of the year.

The River Thames

The village of Hurley, one of the prettiest on the Thames, lies opposite the wooded Buckinghamshire bank. If you are visiting the village for the first time, there are many treats in store, including picturesque Tithecote Manor. Hurley also includes the remains of a Benedictine priory which was established by the Normans in the 11th century. The grounds of the priory were quite extensive and many of the surviving buildings in the village were once part of it. The church was one of these – Editha, sister of Edward the Confessor, is reputed to be buried here – and next to it is a house which was once the monastic refectory.

The walk starts at the Black Boy, a late 16th-century beamed inn which was built as a pub, possibly to serve local farmers and the agricultural community in general. Its history is quite extensive. The 'black boy' in the pub's name, politically unacceptable today, is Charles II, whose skin colour was described as 'very dark and swarthy'. The 17th-century monarch had mixed blood in his veins – a quarter Scottish, Danish, French and Italian – and when he was born his mother, Henrietta Maria of France, indicated to her sister-in-law that she had given birth to a 'black baby' or 'black boy'. It is believed that years later, while he was in France and Cromwell was still ruler, Charles II's followers met secretly at those inns called 'the Black Boy', as they were considered safe houses in which to plot his return to power.

There is a strong emphasis on vegetarian food at the inn, while other dishes include beef stroganoff, fisherman's crumble, grilled prime sirloin steak and scampi. Portuguese and Italian food also feature on the varied menu and battered cod and chips is one of the very popular fish dishes. Real ales include Brakspear Bitter and Mild; Heineken and Guinness are also available. Families are most welcome, but no children under 14 are allowed in the bar. Large parties are advised to book. Outside, there is a 2-acre garden where children can play in safety. Dogs are restricted to the beer garden, or the stable if wet. The Black Boy is open from 11.30 am to 2.30 pm (3 pm on Saturday) and 6 pm to 11 pm on Monday to Saturday, and from 12 noon to 3 pm and 7 pm to 10.30 pm on Sunday. Food is served from 12 noon to 2 pm and 7 pm to 10.45 pm between Monday and Saturday and from 12 noon to 1.45 pm and 7 pm to 9 pm on Sunday. Telephone: 01628 824212.

- **HOW TO GET THERE:** Hurley is just to the north of the A4130, to the west of Maidenhead. The Black Boy is west of the turning to the village.
- **PARKING:** Permission has been given for walking customers to park at the pub and the walk is described from here. Alternatively, use the car park in the centre of Hurley and start the walk at point 3.
- **LENGTH OF THE WALK:** 4 miles. Map: OS Landranger 175 Reading and Windsor (GR 812830).

THE WALK

1. From the front of the inn, turn right and right again, following the signposted 'no through road'. There are paddocks on the left and fields on the right. Pass the entrance to Culham Farms on the left and on the right is a development of stone and flint houses, converted from some

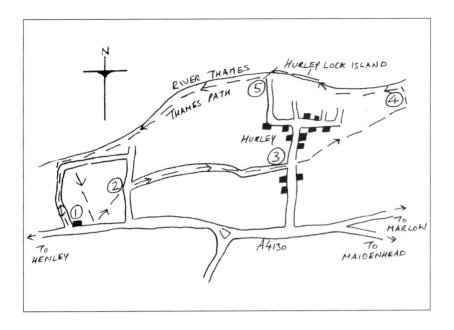

old farm buildings. As the road bends right, go forward on a path to the bank of the Thames. Bear right along the riverside path – the scene is a striking one as the majestic river snakes through the countryside. The walk now follows part of the long-distance Thames Path. Soon the path joins a drive and here there is a junction of ways. Take the right-hand path and follow it between houses. Negotiate a stile and head out across the field, passing under some power cables. There are good views across the well-wooded countryside and hillslopes of the Thames Valley at this early stage of the walk. Look for a stile in the boundary hedge and go diagonally across the next field to a stile leading out to the A4130 road. Do not cross it; instead, follow the path across the field and keep to the left of a house partly enclosed by trees. Walk alongside a hedge, join a drive and make for a road junction.

2. Go straight on, following the single track lane through the trees and keeping a stream on the immediate left. Pass a house partly enclosed by white railings on the left, followed by paddocks, and continue on the road. Disregard a footpath at the entrance to Field House, pass The Croft, Sweet Briar Cottage and the cricket ground on the left.

3. At the road junction you will see the Olde Bell, a famous part-

Hurley Lock Island

timbered hotel and restaurant, located at the heart of Hurley. The 12th-century building, originally a hospice attached to the nearby priory, is one of the loveliest and most historic in the village. There is, reputedly, an underground passage running from the inn to the old crypt. Go straight over to join a path between wooden panel fencing and corrugated iron fencing, enclosed by overhanging trees. Soon the fences give way to trees and undergrowth with views over fields towards occasional houses. Cross a track on a bend and continue on the waymarked path, which can be a little overgrown in places during the summer months. Follow the path alongside a caravan park; cross a stile and join a drive running along the park perimeter. Head towards a backdrop of trees up ahead and cross a concrete stile on the left. Take the path through the trees to the Thames riverbank and turn left.

4. There are tantalizing glimpses of the river between lines of chestnut trees, their branches reaching down to the water's edge. On the opposite bank is a marina and, not surprisingly, that side of the river is usually lined with motor launches and cruisers. Walk through the trees, which are prettily reflected in the water, and cross delightful watermeadows overlooking the river. Go through a kissing gate and then follow the path up over the footbridge leading to Hurley Lock

Island. Pass the lock and the lock keeper's cottage and continue along the towpath, returning to the main bank at the next footbridge.

5. At this point you have a choice. To visit Hurley, go down the steps and follow the tarmac path into the village. To continue the main walk, turn right immediately over the footbridge and follow the Thames Path. Pass a property with its own boathouse on the left and then cross picturesque watermeadows, characterized by grassy expanses and trees. Pass a weir on the right and continue across the meadows. Over to the right, across the river, is the distinctive façade of Danesfield House. The house used to be owned by the MOD but these days it is a hotel. Keep going along the Thames Path. Pass through a gate and follow the path alongside rows of cottages, riverside chalets and timber-framed villas. On reaching the stone and flint barn development, bear left away from the river and retrace your steps to the inn.

PLACES OF INTEREST NEARBY
The Courage Shire Horse Centre on the A4 at Maidenhead Thicket has many attractions, including dray rides, an audio-visual presentation, a gift shop and a small animal and bird area. The site is ideal for a fun-filled family outing. Telephone: 01628 824848.

THAMES VALLEY VIEWS
❧❀☙

North of the Oxfordshire town of Henley and beyond elegant Temple Island, the Thames swings in a wide horseshoe bend to reach Hambleden Lock, one of its key landmarks. Some of the loveliest views of this most famous of rivers are enjoyed on this classic country walk.

Temple Island on the Thames.

Situated amidst Berkshire's lush green meadows and buried deep down winding country lanes, the little village of Aston is worthy of close inspection. There was once a ferry crossing at this point on the Thames. The Flower Pot dates back to 1890 and was built to cater for 'boating parties and fishermen' – as the strikingly decorated sign outside says. With its Victorian character still intact, the inn evokes images of Jerome K. Jerome and *Three Men in a Boat*.

The Flower Pot offers several real ales, including Brakspear Special and Ordinary. Heineken and Stella Artois are also available and wine is served by the glass. Hot and cold bar lunches are served every day and there is a range of sandwiches made from crusty French bread. Game features prominently on the menu, with dishes such as venison, pigeon and rabbit. However, vegetarians are well catered for too, and there is also a selection of fresh fish, including halibut, swordfish steaks and sea bass. The inn is open from 10.30 am until 3 pm and 6 pm until 11 pm between Monday and Saturday. On Sunday the hours are 12 noon until 3 pm and 7 pm until 10.30 pm. Food is served from 12 noon to 2 pm and 6.30 pm to 9 pm; there is no food on Sunday evening in winter. The Flower Pot, which offers bed and breakfast accommodation, also has a large and very popular beer garden with good views over the Thames Valley. Telephone: 01491 574721.

- **HOW TO GET THERE:** Aston is about 1 mile north of the A4130, about 2 miles east of Henley.
- **PARKING:** The Flower Pot is the most suitable place to park. Permission has been given by the landlord for walking customers to park here. Alternatively, park in Remenham and start the walk at point 2.
- **LENGTH OF THE WALK:** 3½ miles. Map: OS Landranger 175 Reading and Windsor (GR 785842).

THE WALK

1. Walk up the lane, heading south towards Remenham Hill. Pass a turning on the left (signposted 'Thames Path') and continue along the lane for a short distance. Turn right immediately beyond Highway Cottage and head up to a stile. Go straight ahead up the rectangular field, join a track and pass alongside power cables and a tongue of woodland. This stretch of the route offers outstanding views across the Thames Valley.

2. Bear right on reaching the road and descend the slope, following the lane beneath overhanging trees. The lane curves to the left and once again there is a classic impression of the valley seen here in all its glory. Merge with another road at the next junction and go straight on to Remenham church, its low, flint tower acting as a famous local landmark. When the road bends left, swing right and pass the lychgate. Follow the lane to the entrance to The Reach; there is a footpath sign and a galvanized gate here. Continue ahead to a kissing gate and emerge onto the Thames riverbank. This stretch of the river is often busy with an assortment of craft - everything from tiny motor boats to palatial cabin cruisers. Turn right and walk along to Temple Island, the

89

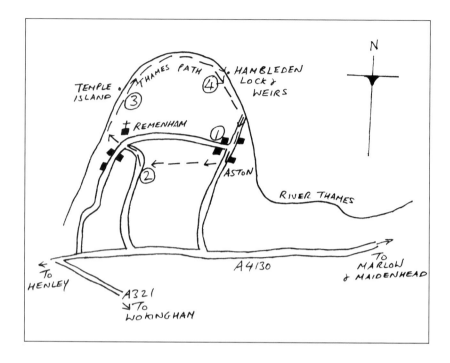

site of an elegant Georgian folly which is the official starting point for the Henley Regatta races. The course is 1 mile and 450 yards long and the world-famous event, an integral part of the British social calendar, takes place in the first week of July.

3. The wooded slopes of the Chiltern Hills rise dramatically on this stretch of the walk, creating a glorious multi-coloured picture – particularly in summer and autumn. Over on the opposite bank is Greenlands, a sumptuous Italianate mansion built in 1853 for W.H. Smith, who later became Viscount Hambleden. Pass Hambleden Lock and look across the weirs here to the weatherboarded façade of Hambleden Mill. Originally driven by a water turbine, the mill was converted into apartments after it ceased operating in the mid 1950s.

4. Follow a track between farmland and the river and when it begins to curve right, go through a gate and follow the Thames Path ahead. The walk now crosses delightful tree-fringed meadows before reaching a kissing gate and footbridge at Aston Ferry. Turn right by the ferry landing and follow a single track lane back to the inn at Aston.

The Flower Pot

PLACES OF INTEREST NEARBY
Henley-on-Thames is a short drive from Aston and includes a number of fine buildings. The central position of its parish church and the rectilinear layout of the town, which can still be traced today, are remnants of medieval planning. Walkers can join the Thames Path at Henley and follow a stretch of it upstream or down. Henley Tourist Information Centre can be reached on 01491 578034. *Greys Court* at Rotherfield Greys is a gabled brick and flint Elizabethan house in the care of the National Trust and open to the public during the summer. Greys Court and the village owe their name to Lord de Grey, who fought at Crécy, became one of the original Knights of the Garter and was given a licence to crenellate the house in 1348. Greys Court includes a Tudor donkey-wheel well house and the garden contains the Archbishop's Maze, whose design is based on the theme of reconciliation. Telephone: 01491 628529.

DISCOVERING DINTON PASTURES:
THE SIX LAKES WALK

Dinton Pastures Country Park comprises about 230 acres of lakes, meadows and picnic areas. The park attracts many visitors who come to walk, fish, picnic and birdwatch. This fascinating walk stays within the boundaries of Dinton Pastures, visiting six different lakes on the way.

Black Swan Lake

The lakes at Dinton Pastures were once gravel workings which were flooded to form the focal point of an attractive recreational country park. The park, which has an information centre, exhibition room, children's play area and three birdwatching hides, takes its name from the dairy farm that once occupied this site. The farmhouse still survives and includes a popular teashop. The largest of the lakes at Dinton Pastures is Black Swan and the Emm Brook once flowed where the lake is now situated. It was later diverted and the oaks on the island in the lake were once on the banks of the stream. Tufted duck, herring gull, tern and great crested grebe are among the different species of bird to be found here. For more information, telephone: 0118 9342016.

The Tea Cosy café overlooks a pleasant garden with several tables to enable you to enjoy your refreshments outside. There are appetizing cakes, cream teas and toasted teacakes. Ploughman's lunches, jacket potatoes and other meals such as ham, egg and chips are on offer at lunchtime. The Tea Cosy is open for business between 10 am and 4 pm throughout the year. Telephone: 0118 9321071.

- **HOW TO GET THERE:** The country park is off the B3030 (Davis Street), about 1 mile south-west of the village of Hurst, which is on the A321 Wokingham to Henley road.
- **PARKING:** There is plenty of room to park in the main car park. If you prefer, begin at the car park at Sandford Mill copse, picking up the walk at point 3.
- **LENGTH OF THE WALK:** 3 miles. Map: OS Landranger 175 Reading and Windsor (GR 784717).

THE WALK

1. Keep the Tea Cosy café and Countryside Service office on the right and High Chimneys behind you and go through the gate by the large map of the site. Follow the wide path between undergrowth and trees, merge with another path and then cross the Emm Brook. Beyond the bridge, where the path forks, veer right at the sign 'Dogs on lead - picnic area'. Pass an enclosed play area on the left, keep the Emm Brook on the right and now there are tantalizing glimpses of Black Swan Lake up ahead. Swing left on reaching the water and follow the path beside bulrushes with good views of the lake. When the path veers right turn left and cross a bridge by an information board. Turn right here and then swing left at the fork (signposted 'River Loddon'). Keep to the main track with White Swan Lake on your right. Bear left at the point where a flight of steps is seen on the left. This path takes you to a lake known as Tufty's Corner.

2. Follow the path through the trees and when you reach a junction turn right and keep the River Loddon on your left. Walk along to the next bridge. Do not cross it; instead keep on along the riverside path. White Swan Lake lies over to the right, glimpsed at intervals between the trees. Further on, the path curves to the right, in line with the river,

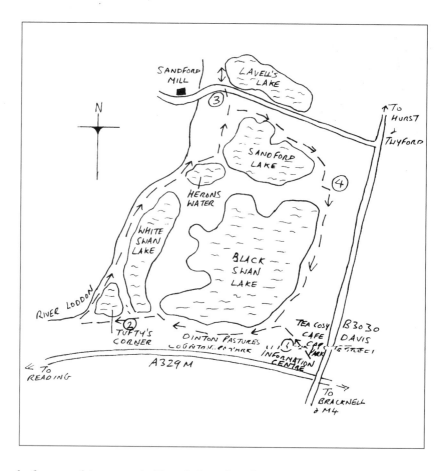

before reaching a track. Turn left and walk alongside Herons Water to a sign for 'Sandford Lake, Black Swan Lake and Lavell's Lake – Conservation Area'. Turn left and keep Sandford Lake on the right, noting its islets dotted about in the middle. When the path curves right go out to the road by an information board.

3. The white weatherboarded façade of Sandford Mill can be seen along to the left. Turn right for several steps, then go through the kissing gate by the footpath sign. Keep left at the fork and follow the sign for the Teal hide, which overlooks the wader scrapes. The scrapes are used by wading birds, including the green sandpiper and redshank, whilst here on migration. The hide features illustrations of the birds you are likely to see at Lavell's Lake. This site is for serious ornithologists.

94

Sandford Mill

Not long ago this corner of the park was a meadow grazed by cattle or cut for hay, though the landscape changed dramatically at the time of gravel extraction. Retrace your steps to the road, cross over and return to the lakeside path. Continue with Sandford Lake on your right; on reaching a sign – 'Sandford Lake – wildlife area – dogs under control' – veer left over a bridge and turn left.

4. Black Swan Sailing Club can be seen on the left. Continue on the wide stony path and look across the lake to Goat Island, noted for its population of goats. On reaching the picnic area overlooking Black Swan Lake, turn left and retrace your steps back to the main car park.

PLACES OF INTEREST NEARBY
The Berkshire Museum of Aviation at Mohawk Way, on the northern edge of Dinton Pastures country park, is dedicated to the contribution the county has made to flying. A Second World War hangar has been moved here from Woodley and there are various aircraft representing Berkshire aviation over the last 60 years. The museum is open from March to October on Wednesday, Saturday and Sunday, as well as bank holidays, between 10.30 am and 5 pm and from noon until 4 pm on Sundays in winter. Telephone: 0118 9448089.